W9-DCC-128

Congregational Discipling

A Three Fold Vision for Worship, Community, and Mission

sponsored by
Mennonite Board of Congregational Ministries
Elkhart, Indiana
Herald Press Congregational Publishing
Scottdale, Pennsylvania
of the Mennonite Church, Elkhart, Indiana

Commission on Education
Newton, Kansas
of the General Conference Mennonite Church,
Newton, Kansas

Herald Press
Scottdale, Pennsylvania
Waterloo, Ontario

Library of Congress Cataloging-in-Publication Data

Congregational discipling : a threefold vision for worship, community, and mission / sponsored by Mennonite Board of Congregational Ministries, Elkhart, Indiana.
  p. cm.
  ISBN 0-8361-9450-0 (alk. paper)
  1. Church. 2. Mission of the church. 3. Discipling (Christianity) 4. Mennonites—Doctrines. 5. Anabaptists— Doctrines.   I. Mennonite Board of Congregational Ministries
BX8128.C49C66   1997
289.7'3—dc21   97-12503

The paper used in this publication is recycled and meets the minimum requirements of American National Standard for Information Sciences—Permanence of Paper for Printed Library Materials, ANSI Z39.48-1984.

Scripture Quotations are from the New Revised Standard Version, Copyright © 1989 by the Division of Christian Education of the National Council of Churches of Christ in the USA and are used by permission.

CONGREGATIONAL DISCIPLING: A THREE FOLD VISION FOR WORSHIP, COMMUNITY, AND MISSION
Copyright © 1997 by Herald Press, Scottdale, Pa. 15683
All rights reserved
Printed in the United States of America
Library of Congress Catalog Number: 97-12503
International Standard Book Number: 0-8361-9450-0
Book and cover design by James M. Butti

1 2 3 4 5 6 7 8 9 10 01 00 99 98 97

L. Kaufmann

Congregational Discipling

The Great Commandments

One of the scribes asked Jesus, *"Which commandment is the first of all?"*

Jesus answered, *"The first is,*
'Hear, O Israel: the Lord our God, the Lord is one; you shall love the Lord your God with all your heart, and with all your soul, and with all your strength.'"
"The second is this,
'You shall love your neighbor as yourself".
"There is no other commandment greater than these."
—Mark 12:29-31

Contents

Foreword

Congregational life is at the center of our Anabaptist/ Mennonite understanding of the church. As a pastor of twenty-three years, I read this book with interest.

The result of much diligent work by dedicated and gifted servants in the church, the book impresses us with its admonition to view our congregation through the lens of a focused purpose. Congregational Life must afford us a wholistic view of ourselves as servants of Christ. It invites us to share our knowledge of God's grace and leading beyond our fellowship through mission. The book offers valuable instruction on the methods of ministry in congregations toward these ends.

The calling of the pastor is implicit, I noted, not explicit throughout the work. While it is proper to affirm the diversity of leadership functions in congregations, as the book does so well, it is my view that the focused leadership of pastors remains an essential element of congregational life. In addition, as I used to tell pastoral interns of college and seminary age, "It is who you are much more than what you will do in ministry that will count."

Amidst all the helpful advice on methods and structures found throughout the book, the reader may wish to keep in mind that ministry has been vested in people, not only in functions. In healthy, ministering congregations, the elements of confident leadership are combined with genuine humility. Personal risk taking, when combined with open collaboration with others, forms a mysterious bond between leaders and followers in congregations. This results in a strange enabling power of the Gospel that waits to be released through each member in the congregation.

May this book enlighten you. But even more, may it cause the reader to reexamine themselves and to nurture their own strengths of leadership for the sake of Christ's cause.

James Schrag, General Secretary
General Conference Mennonite Church

I well remember sitting in a steamy Allegheny Mennonite Conference delegate session on a July day as the Mennonite Board of Congregational Ministries gave its report at our annual conference sessions. All of the participants were captivated by the "performance" which effectively made the point of the church as community with each of the parts adding a distinctive and necessary part to the whole. The fact that we were then encouraged to sample the resulting product simply served to drive the point deeper into my consciousness.

Years have passed since that demonstration and, while I can no longer savor the flavor of the gorp, the image of the church as community has become richer and sweeter as the years have passed. This book helps to carry the message that so enriched my life several years ago. By connecting the idea of the church as community with the concept of mission and worship each of these elements of the trifoliar takes on new meaning and strength. I especially appreciate the central function of the formation of disciples in the midst of that trifoliar.

May God bless this "recipe" to the enrichment and sustenance of the church of Jesus Christ.

George B. Stoltzfus, General Secretary
Mennonite Church

Chapter 1

A Recipe for Healthy Congregations

by Marlene Kropf

A man appears on stage in a chef's hat and apron carrying a wooden spoon in one hand and a large mixing bowl in the other. Conference delegates look up expectantly. All morning they have listened to reports and speeches. They have voted and taken actions. By now they are a little weary of business and are looking forward to a break.

What is he saying? He has a recipe for healthy congregational life?

Slowly the man opens a box of raisins and drops them into the mixing bowl. They stick together, so he nudges them apart. "It's like the church," the man says. "The church is a community of people who love each other and care for each other. Sometimes they stick together so much it's hard to separate them."

A woman in a chef's apron steps up and adds a bag of multicolored M&M's to the mixture. "The church would be pretty dull if it were only raisins," she says as she stirs. "The church is a community that worships God. M&M's represent the vertical dimension of congregational life— the sweetness of worship as we pray, sing, and listen to the Word as well as the colorful diversity of all ages and groups of people meeting God together."

She is interrupted by another man also wearing a chef's apron. "One thing more is needed," he says. "Though this is an attractive mixture, it lacks salt." He pours in a jar of salty peanuts and begins to stir. "The church is salt in the world—a people engaged in mission. When we share our faith with others, make peace, and serve those in need, we fulfill the call of Jesus to make disciples."

The first man lifts up the bowl and shows the conference delegates the colorful, tasty mixture the chefs have made. "This is what the church tastes like," he says. "Have a handful!"

All across Canada and the United States, regional and area Mennonite conferences/districts and local congregations have been eating GORP, the culinary representation of the Congregational Discipling Vision. This recipe has been served to thousands of people.

Recipe for GORP*
To serve 50 people, mix the following:
  2 lbs. of raisins
  1 lb. of plain M&M's (not peanut M&M's)
  1 lb. of **salted** peanuts

  * acronym for "Good Old Raisins and Peanuts"

Where does the Congregational Discipling Vision come from? And how did it become a GORP recipe? Perhaps the place to begin is with Jesus and the great commandment.

Foundation for a Vision

One day a thoughtful adult came to Jesus and said, "I'd like an answer, Jesus. When you get to the heart of the matter, when you focus on what is absolutely essential, what does God really want from us? What does it mean for humans to be in relationship with God? What does healthy spirituality look like?"

The answer of Jesus was simple but profound:
Love the Lord your God with all your heart,
and with all your soul,
and with all your mind,
and with all your strength.
And love your neighbor as yourself.
(Mark 12:28-34)

That's it—the sum of the gospel. In just two sentences, Jesus cut through complex religious ideas and practices and identified what is the heart of faith. To love God, to love one's self (and by extension, one's people or community), and to love the neighbor (and by extension, all peoples everywhere) is the secret of a virtuous and fruitful life.

What's more, Jesus gave his followers the ministry of continuing his work of calling people to fulfill God's dream of a loving world. Near the end of his life, Jesus prayed, "As you have sent me into the world, so I have sent them into the world" (John 17:18). In his farewell address, Jesus said:
Going therefore,
make disciples of all nations,
baptizing them in the name of the Father and the Son
and the Holy Spirit,
teaching them to observe all that I have commanded you.
(Matthew 28:19-20, literal translation from the Greek by Jacob W. Elias, Elkhart, Indiana.)

The disciple-making task, according to Jesus, is twofold:

First, to call people to faith and baptize them in the name of the triune God and

Second, to teach them to observe all things that Jesus commanded—that is, to love God, self, and neighbor—and come to mature faith.

Every generation faces the question of how to live the heart of the Christian gospel and how to pass it on.

Although the words of Jesus are simple and clear, fulfilling them requires great courage and creativity. When a child is born, parents struggle with the question: How can we teach our child to love God, self, and neighbor? The same question is asked when the church forms new Christians in their faith. Many competing influences attempt to subvert or destroy our efforts. A violent, competitive world persuades children, youth, and adults to become ruthless and self-centered. In the midst of affluence and materialism, people learn to desire power and possessions more than God. Under the influences of contemporary culture, many struggle to find the wholeness Jesus describes.

The Church: God's Gift for Growth

Passing on the Christian faith is not meant to be the task of parents or teachers or pastors alone. Much more is needed in our complex world. Instead of a lonely leadership task, passing on faith and nurturing people to become whole in Christ is the work of the entire faith community. The church is meant to be a gift for our growth toward God. Whether we are young people, middle-aged, or older adults, the church is God's provision for our ongoing transformation into Christlikeness. Learning to love is a lifelong process which is accomplished only as we participate in the body of Christ.

The church, however, is also a fragile institution. In many places at the end of the twentieth century, biblical faith is an endangered phenomenon. In her book *A History of God* (Alfred A. Knopf, 1993), British scholar Karen Armstrong concludes that the twentieth century is the only age in history that has not regarded some form of faith as natural and normative. In addition, the social institutions which formerly worked together toward similar goals are often no longer seen as supportive of each other.

Before World War II, for example, many parents depended upon the extended family, friends, public schools, media, summer camp, youth organizations, the church, and small-town values to communicate a similar priority of loving God and neighbor. In our pluralistic culture, these assumptions no longer hold together. Instead of being a center of values, the church competes with other institutions and movements for the loyalty and devotion of members. Thus the process of forming faith is dangerously fragmented and weakened.

In such a time, it becomes imperative for Christians to look carefully at the church and answer these questions:

First, What makes a healthy church?

Second, What kind of vision for congregational life will sustain the body of Christ and will make it a dynamic center of growth?

Third, How can the church fulfill its purpose of calling people to love God, self, and neighbor?

A Fresh Look

This book takes a fresh look at the church. Rooted in a decade of intensive testing, writing, and teaching, the Congregational Discipling Vision described in this volume is the joint effort of congregational, area conference, and denominational leaders of the General Conference Mennonite Church and the Mennonite Church (see Appendix 1 for the story of how the Vision was developed). This vision takes into account biblical teachings and Anabaptist understandings about the nature of the church as well as the realities of contemporary culture. This vision for renewal can guide the church into the twenty-first century. What is offered is a simple, sturdy theology of congregational life that provides a framework for living the great commandment: to love God, self and neighbor.

Chapter 2

Three Essential Arenas of Common Life: Worship, Community, and Mission

by Marlene Kropf

Introduction

If love of God, self and neighbor is the sum of the gospel, what kind of church is needed to form people who will live out the gospel? By now, the answer seems fairly obvious. Such a church holds a vision of love at its center and creates structures to form and express that love to God, self, and neighbor.

Historically, the church has carried out Jesus' vision of love in three essential, interdependent dimensions or arenas of congregational life: **worship, community**, and **mission**. These correlate with the three points of focus of the Great Commandment. In worship we learn to love God; in our communal life we learn to love ourselves and each other; and in mission we learn to love our neighbors as God does.

As the church goes about the ordinary business of being the church, a process of formation and transformation naturally occurs in which God's Spirit faithfully creates a people who love God, self, and neighbor. Though each of the three arenas of congregational life is distinct, each one overlaps the other two. Chapters 3, 4, and 5 explore each of the arenas of action separately and identify their unique potential for the formation and transformation of disciples.

Diagram A

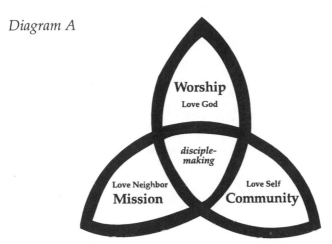

Worship:

In worship, the church enters into God's presence and opens itself to the source of its being. Through Scripture, prayer, ritual, proclamation, offerings, music, the arts, and silence, worshipers are shaped and formed into a faithful covenant community by the story of God's acts in human history, their experience of God's love and power, and their hope in the coming reign of God.

Community:

In community, participants enter into and are nourished by relationships through which transformation into Christlikeness occurs. This arena includes one-to-one, group or family relationships, school settings, camps, the congregation, regional conferences, or the denomination. As Christians learn to trust, forgive, give and receive counsel, and care for others, the discipling community takes on the character of Jesus.

Mission:

In mission, the church answers the call to unite with God's loving, creative, liberating purposes in the world. The church receives gifts of the Spirit, discerns both personal and congregational direction, and commits itself in loving obedience to ministries of evangelism, stewardship, service, peace, and justice.

Congregational Checkup

In your leadership team or discussion group, consider the following activities and questions:

1. Just for fun, give each member of your group three pieces of different-colored clay (Play-Doh works fine). Ask them to create a three-segmented critter that represents the three arenas of congregational life in your church. Use a different color of clay for each arena (perhaps blue for worship, red for community, and green for mission). Let the size of each segment represent the importance or health of that arena. Encourage the group to work in silence until all have completed the task.

2. Invite class members to show their critters to the group. Compare the critters. Do people agree as to which is the most important or healthiest arena? Which is least important? If not, why not?

3. Do these visual images reflect the stated priorities of your congregation? In other words, is the congregation's vision congruent or consistent with that which the clay critters depict? Why or why not?

For further reading and study:

Liberating the Church & Kingdom by Howard A. Snyder. InterVarsity Press, 1983.

Chapter 3

How Do Formation and Transformation Occur in the Congregation's Life of Worship?

by Marlene Kropf

We are all there on Sunday morning—children, teens, middle-aged folks and grandparents—committed Christians and those not yet committed. We meet to worship God.

Worship is such a powerful setting for Christian formation and transformation because our own desire for God is magnified as we join others in seeking God's presence. For an hour or two each week, we lay aside our unique, individual concerns and become a community that encounters God together. As we sing, pray, listen to the Word, affirm our faith, and give our offerings, we join in the universal praise of God. Within the harmony and unity of a circle created by Christ's love, our hearts are renewed and transformed by a fresh outpouring of God's Spirit.

Walter Brueggemann, Old Testament scholar and teacher, says that in worship we are engaged in "world-making." By this he means that through our words and actions in worship we create a world of meaning. We construct a vision of reality—a perspective, not only about what is now, but also of what can be through the power of the Holy Spirit. For a few hours each week, we live as though the reign of God has fully come.

Discipled by the Actions of Worship

By looking carefully at the various acts of worship, we discover a multitude of ways each one contributes to the growing faith and maturity of worshipers who gather each week. At the center of Christian worship is an encounter with the Word of God—both the living Word (the presence of the risen Christ among us) and the written Word of Scripture. As the Scriptures are read and proclaimed, we come to understand who God is and what God's purposes are in the world. With our hearts we feel the tug of God's love and respond in faith and devotion.

Formed by Story and Preaching

The church is a story-formed community. We receive our identity from the stories we hear of God's action through history. Through the lives of biblical characters or heroes of faith, we catch glimpses of who we are to become. Because stories have such power to shape our imagination and values, it is crucial that Bible stories be told well.

In *To a Dancing God; Notes of a Spiritual Traveler* (Harper/San Francisco 1990, pp. 8-9), Sam Keen reflects: "It was in Tennessee that I first learned the history of my native land. Before I was six, I had walked through Judea, Galilee, Capernaum, Bethlehem, and Jerusalem, sharing a dusty road with Jesus and the disciples, finding at day's end the comfort of a footbath, bread and olives in a humble home. And what a rich time and place it was to which I belonged! Over these hills and desert places, my forebears roamed. From papier-mâché models, I learned the architecture of the Holy Land, and from bathrobe dramas its way of dress (and at recess there was milk and graham crackers). I learned of Deborah's heroism (but not of Molly Pitcher's) and of the judges and kings the Lord raised to lead and chastise his people (but not of the judges of Blount County who helped to keep whiskey illegal and bootlegging profitable). I knew the topography of Judea before I could locate the Cumberland Plateau, as I knew the road from Damascus to Jerusalem before I could find my way from Maryville to Knoxville."

As the Word is proclaimed in preaching, the congregation is shaped and formed in faith, hope, and love. Though one sermon rarely transforms a church, thoughtfully preached sermons over time transform the church's character. For example, a pastor's oft-repeated images of God tend to shape the way a congregation thinks and feels about God and responds to God's call. If a pastor's own images of God are well-rounded and include God's love and mercy as well as God's holiness and judgment, then the congregation's understanding and experience of God will also be healthy and biblical.

Nourished by Singing

The Word of God is proclaimed in more ways than words alone. Perhaps the most important way many worshipers hear the Word is through songs and hymns. Hymn texts bring the words of Scripture to life, establish them in our hearts, and shape our responses to God as well as our witness in the world. It is no exaggeration to say that the theological convictions of a congregation are formed as much by songs as by sermons, confessions of faith, or creeds.

Music is more than its texts. Sound and melody become a gateway to the presence of God. Whether we sing in unison or in harmony as we offer praise and confession to God, worshipers often find themselves transported beyond time and space into an encounter with a merciful and majestic God.

Enlightened by the Arts

Music is only one artistic medium that brings worshipers into God's presence. Sometimes such breathtaking moments also occur when we see a drama or dance. A sense of God's presence can also happen when a painting or piece of sculpture is incorporated into the visual environment of worship.

In one congregation when a drama of the parable of the prodigal son (Luke 15:11-32) was enacted, people saw the welcoming face of God more powerfully than they had ever seen it before. Joy was awakened in another congregation when children danced as frisky sheep in God's pasture during a reading of Psalm 100. On Pentecost Sunday, in a third congregation, a pastor displayed a stone sculpture titled simply, "Spirit." The contours and open spaces of the sculpture revealed the mystery of the Spirit's presence as an always moving, never-contained expression of God's activity in the world.

Transformed by Prayer

Prayer is another element of worship that forms and transforms God's people. In prayer, we encounter God most directly. As creatures we listen to God's still, small voice. We also dare to address the Maker of the universe. In *Holy the Firm*, Annie Dillard (Harper/Collins, 1988, p. 59) remarks humorously but truthfully; "I often think of the set pieces of liturgy as certain words which people have successfully addressed to God without their getting killed."

What we pray and how we pray influences who we become. For example, when the intercessory prayers of the congregation are offered, not only for the sick and wounded ones nearby, but also include universal concerns such as victims of drought or war, then the congregation begins to experience the breadth of God's vision. The good news is not just for us and our kind but for "every creature in heav-

en and on earth and under the earth, and on the sea, and all
that is in them" (Revelation 5:13).

Empowered by Giving

The act of giving an offering reminds us each week that
all we are and have belongs to God. When we sing or hear
joyful music as we give our money or "dance the offering
to the altar" (as African Christians do), we offer praise to
our generous God. We also discover that our bondage to
money and all it buys is broken. We are set free to live with
mercy and compassion in God's world.

Fashioned by Rituals

The rituals and ceremonies of the church play key roles
in forming faith. As new believers are baptized and enter
the community of faith, all members of the congregation
are invited to renew their baptismal vows, experience
again the joy of cleansing grace, and reaffirm their
covenant with Jesus Christ. In celebrating the Lord's
Supper, the congregation enters into a profound experience
of union with Christ and with each other. Through the
symbols of bread and wine, we remember God's acts of
deliverance. We look forward to the great feast at which all
nations and peoples will gather at the marriage supper of
the Lamb.

Influenced by Space

The architectural space in which congregations meet
contributes to the way worshipers encounter God and to
their formation as Christians. Because light is such a primary symbol of God's presence, shafts of light can open
people to a deeper awareness of the mystery of God. How
well worshipers see and hear each other affects their sense
of community. The design and quality of materials reflect
the congregation's commitment to justice and simplicity.

Shaped by Participation

The way we lead worship and who directs or participates also shapes people's faith. When women, men, young people, and children actively join in worship, we are, in effect, teaching about who belongs in God's reign. If worship leaders choose words with care and with an ear for beauty, they communicate their reverence for and delight in God. The use of current language rather than obsolete or old-fashioned styles also encourages people to approach God. Language that includes and welcomes women and men, young and old, poor and rich, or people of many colors and cultures is also formative in worship.

Thus weekly worship is an opportunity for the congregation to live out the reality of God's new reign—the just and peaceful community of those whose lives are centered in Christ. As we see this new reality on Sunday, we are formed and shaped in a vision for how to live our lives all week long.

Discipled by Worship Leading

In addition to the actions of worship, members are also discipled as they participate in worship leadership. The gifts of worshipers are developed and strengthened as they sing in choirs, read Scripture, act in dramas, create banners, or tell a story to children. Each congregation needs to find ways to discover and nourish the many gifts needed for worship.

A Virginia pastor works intentionally to teach young people to pray in public by inviting them to assist her in praying the pastoral prayer. On Saturday afternoon, she meets with a young person to discuss what might be included in the pastoral prayer. She mentions people in the congregation who are in need of prayer; they talk about situations in the community and the wider world. The young person decides the concerns about which he or she wants to pray. Together they craft a prayer.

The next morning in worship, the pastor begins the pastoral prayer; then the young person prays; and finally the pastor concludes the prayer. Beyond learning to function as a leader of prayer, these young people are also being schooled in compassion as they learn to care for members of the church and others in need.

The very process of planning worship can also be an experience of discipling. As songleaders, musicians, worship leaders, and preachers open themselves to Scripture and listen to God's voice as they prepare, they will find themselves being transformed by the Spirit. Even at the times when worship does not seem to work, when all the best planning falls apart and leaders feel humiliated, even then powerful learning can occur.

It is God's Spirit who moves the hearts of worshipers, not the careful plans of human leaders or skillful preachers. Sometimes worship leaders need to discover that God uses even imperfect planning or flawed leading.

Discipled by Welcoming Others to Worship

Congregations that catch a vision for making disciples will also be alert to the ways seekers and visitors experience the presence and call of Christ in worship. In fact, the discipling of seekers begins before they join the congregation in worship.

By choosing the right people as "up-fronters" (those who have the gifts of friendliness, hospitality, and service), a congregation invites seekers and strangers by the attention and actions of greeters, church hosts or hostesses, and ushers who go the second mile.

John Maxwell, pastor of a growing church in San Diego, California, says that some of the most important people in the worship service are the visitor, the parking lot attendant, the greeter, the nursery worker, the usher, and even the congregational member next to whom a visitor sits! The pastor comes tenth on his list. That's because visitors usually decide if they will return to that church within the first ten minutes after they enter the parking lot.

As these workers welcome and include people—adults, youth, and children—they themselves grow in faith in ways never experienced before. The perfunctory duties of meeting strangers, such as shaking hands, smiling, giving a welcome packet, and asking people's names, all have the potential to shape their skills for service and witness. An initial encounter may even open a way to go beyond the bounds of mere sociability to develop a lasting friendship. At the least, greeters may see their own warmth and openness being reciprocated by visitors. This ministry of welcoming strangers at the church door may plant a new seed within a disciple that will flourish and bear fruit in other ministries of witness and evangelism.

Worshipers experience the discipling power of the gospel in the midst of the weekly gathering. Those who lead others into the presence of God also discover their own spirits being enlivened. As the Christian community gathers to meet God in worship, faith is formed, lives are transformed, and power is poured out upon God's people. They then go out to love and serve God in the world.

Congregational Checkup

In your leadership team or discussion group, consider the following questions:

1. How have you experienced worship as a setting for formation and transformation in your congregation?

a. What stories can you tell about a sermon that spoke powerfully to you? A song that moved you or revealed to you a fresh vision of Christ? A presentation of Scripture that revealed something new? A piece of art that opened your eyes?

b. How has prayer shaped faith in worship?

c. What images of God are typical in your worship setting? Are some images overused? Are others neglected? Why?

d. How is a well-rounded diet of Scripture provided for reading and proclamation in worship?

e. What have you discovered about God by participating in a baptismal or communion service?

f. In what ways does the offering invite people in your congregation to offer all they are and have to God?

g. What does the architecture of your meetinghouse say about your congregation's view of God? About who you are as a congregation? About your mission in the world?

h. What vision of the reign of God is communicated by the choice of worship leaders and how worship is conducted in your congregation?

i. What kind of welcome to worship do strangers and seekers receive in your congregation?

2. What changes are needed to enhance and expand the discipling potential of worship in your congregation? How will you begin to make these changes? Who can help to implement such changes?

For further reading and study:

The School of the Church: Worship and Christian Formation by Philip H. Pfatteicher. Trinity Press International, 1995.

Real Worship: It Will Transform Your Life by Warren W. Wiersbe. Thomas Nelson, 1986.

Meeting God Through Worship by Anne Broyles. Abingdon Press, 1992.

Participating in Worship: History, Theory and Practice by Craig Douglas Erickson. Westminister/John Knox, 1989.

Enter His Gates: Fitting Worship Together by Eleanor Kreider. Herald Press, 1990.

Communion Shapes Character, by Eleanor Kreider, Herald Press, 1997.

Worship and Evangelism in Pre-Christendom by Alan Kreider. Grove Books, Ltd., 1995.

Chapter 4

How Do Formation and Transformation Occur in the Congregation's Life of Community?

by Marlene Kropf

As the congregation worships God together, faith is formed and shaped. Lives are transformed. Beyond the arena of worship, the relationships and interactions that occur within the body of Christ are another essential arena for discipling. As Christians encourage each other and care for and serve one another, they become more and more like Jesus. If they hurt or grieve another, they seek forgiveness and reconciliation. As a healthy organism, the church grows together in love and unity. It reflects the love of Christ in the world.

Discipled by Relationships in the Body of Christ

When we Mennonites leave our homes on Sunday morning, we say we're going to "church." When Catholics leave their homes on Sunday morning, they say they're going to "mass." When Muslims leave their homes on Friday morning, they say they're going to "prayers." Does it make any difference where we are going or what we call it?

What if Mennonites said we're going to "worship" on Sunday morning? Would that be different from saying we're going to "church"?

Perhaps there is a difference.

"Church," as we ordinarily use the word, has to do with the human community that gathers in the name of Jesus. If we say we're going to "worship," we emphasize the vertical dimension of congregational life—the first arena. By saying we go to "church," Mennonites emphasize the horizontal dimension of congregational life.

The experience of interdependent relationships in community has a high value for Mennonites. Partly because of our theological convictions and partly because of our history of close-knit ethnic communities, Mennonites have been attracted to the image of "family" to describe the church. In the past instead of using honorary titles or formal address in the church, we simply called each other "brother" and "sister." In today's world of high mobility and cultural pluralism, such a rich heritage still provides a firm foundation for congregational life.

Within the context of a multitude of relationships in the church, faith is formed by guidance as well as by mutual address and confrontation. Parents have the first opportunity to model a life of faith for their children and to teach them the ways of Christ. Grandparents and other relatives as well as siblings also share in passing on faith.

As children are taught the stories of the Christian faith, introduced to prayer and other spiritual practices, encouraged to be generous, and mentored in peacemaking and service, their hearts are opened to the presence of a loving God. Along the way, as they are given opportunity to express childlike faith through the arts—singing, acting, dancing, painting,—the faith of the heart is nurtured. As children come to maturity, they are invited to make their own choice to become disciples of Jesus Christ and to become part of the church and its ministry in the world.

Beyond the family, mentors and teachers exert a powerful influence on the faith development of children and young people. In one congregation a high school senior was having trouble deciding where to go to college. He had received a four-year tuition scholarship from a private men's school and a much smaller scholarship from a church college. Because he would need to pay his own college tuition expenses, he faced a severe internal conflict in making the decision. Should he go to the church college and be nurtured in his own faith tradition even though the costs were considerably higher, or should he make a financially prudent decision and attend the secular school?

Although his parents had listened to his questions and tried to help him come to a resolution, he remained undecided. When his mentor in the congregation learned of the dilemma, he volunteered to take a day off from work, go along to visit the colleges, and offer his assistance in making the decision. After the visit, the mentor and the teenager evaluated what they had learned and made a decision; the student chose the church college.

Walking with others in the church and offering guidance when needed is an important form of discipling. Often such guidance occurs informally in the form of friendships and small groups or more formally in specifically focused ministries such as spiritual friendship or mentoring. As members practice the priestly ministries of caring for one another, praying for each other, discerning together, forgiving each other, and practicing accountability for spiritual growth, they are strengthened as disciples. John Westerhoff once said, "We don't have to like the people in our community of faith; we just have to be willing to die for them!" Such love and commitment to each other's good is a true mark of mature Christian disciples.

An effective setting for discipling through relationships is the church camping program. Countless children and teens have been inspired to love and follow Christ by the example of camp counselors and leaders as well as by relationships with other campers. Twenty-four-hour-a-day modeling is a powerful stimulus for growth.

Another way faith is shaped and formed is through the ministry of teaching. Perhaps the primary gift of teachers as disciplers is to create a hospitable space where learning can occur. In faith formation, the goal is not to communicate a particular body of knowledge (though information is certainly important) but to open the way for learners to grow in love of Christ, neighbor, and self. Educational methods which lead to transformation undergird the discipling process (This topic is discussed further in chapters 6 and 7).

Still other ministries such as spiritual guidance, healing, pastoral care and counseling, and conflict resolution are also arenas for discipling. In the midst of grief or pain, when making decisions, or when facing conflict, many people reach out for a deeper relationship with God. As the church listens to their stories, surrounds them with love, upholds them in prayer, and offers skillful guidance, seekers are transformed. They discover new dimensions of being disciple-followers of Christ. Often these wounded ones then become healers who guide others to wholeness.

The role of leaders is critical in the Christian community. Pastors and elders or deacons have a special responsibility as spiritual guides of the community as a whole. As they preach, preside as priests in the rituals of the church, care for relationships within the body, and proclaim a vision of God's love for the whole world, they represent Christ. They also call the body of Christ to faithfulness and maturity. Their ministry is foundational in the formation of love for God, self, and neighbors.

Discipled by the Story

In addition to the nurture and cultivation of relationships in the body of Christ, another dimension of discipling in the community arena occurs as the story of faith is told. Because the Christian community receives its identity from a story, a primary task of the church is to be a story-keeper and a storyteller. Biblical stories, the stories of the early church and the church throughout history, as well as the stories of a local faith community stir our imagination. They provide a cast of characters who show us how to live as God's people in the world.

More than abstract theological teaching or persuasive argument, the stories of God's actions throughout history shape our vision of who God is and who we are in relationship with God. They provide a framework for character formation, for everyday decision making, and for ethical discernment. Understanding the history of the church also establishes a foundation for analysis of current movements in the church It provides perspective for decision-making.

Discipled by Values and Practices

Not only are the values of a community passed on through stories, they are also communicated through particular practices. The Mennonite heritage of singing, for example, has powerfully bonded its people together. A story is told of Mennonite college students who went to China to study and serve for a semester. After some weeks abroad, they sent home an urgent request for copies of a Mennonite hymnal. They said that without their hymns they did not know who they were in a strange land.

Still another practice that bonds a community is eating together. Gathering around the refreshment table or sitting down to well-laden tables at church potlucks is a favored way of nourishing relationships in the body of Christ. Even here the community continues its discipling ministries. How well children, young people, newcomers, the poor, or strangers are included reflects the quality of love within the body. People naturally feel more comfortable eating with their friends. But when members reach out beyond their comfortable circles and welcome others, they not only offer Christ's love to others, they also grow in their love of Christ.

Mutual aid is another practice that disciples the Christian community. A young family faced numerous expensive medical procedures when their third child was born with a defective heart. When their congregation assisted them with childcare, provided meals, gave them a love offering, and transported them to and from the regional medical center, the family saw the face of Jesus. They felt the love of Christ in new ways. Their faith was deepened. They found strength to endure uncertainties and disruptions. Economic sharing, assisting each other with technical skills and professional expertise, or simple everyday generosity make love visible.

Finally, the church as a community shapes faith as it responds to diversity. Whether it is varying worship styles, differing expectations arising from culture or social class, gender battles, or conflicts between generations, the capacity of the church to care for and respond to the uniqueness of individuals and groups is critical in discipling the community.

Perhaps nothing damages the credibility of the body of Christ more effectively in contemporary culture than racist attitudes and behavior. When Christians of different races and cultures worship and work together in harmony, respecting and valuing each other's differences, they become a powerful sign of the gracious and inclusive reign of God. The love of Christ is revealed as a source of transformation, not only for the church, but for the world.

The apostle Paul says, "But now in Christ Jesus you who were once far off have been brought near by the blood of Christ. For he is our peace; in his flesh he has made both groups into one and has broken down the dividing wall, that is, the hostility between us . . . that he might create in himself one new humanity in place of the two, thus making peace, and might reconcile both groups to God in one body through the cross." (Ephesians 2:13-14, 15b-16a)

Day in and day out, the community of faith makes disciples. No matter what the church is being or doing, it always influences others toward Christ or away from that commitment. Growth in love is ultimately the responsibility of the Holy Spirit. To the church is given the wondrous opportunity to join with God's creative, transforming work; to serve as midwife in the birth of new Christians; and to nurture the ongoing growth of mature followers of Christ.

Congregational Checkup

In your leadership team or discussion group, consider the following questions:

1. How have you experienced the life of the faith community as a setting for formation and transformation in your congregation?

a. What stories can you tell of parents, mentors, and teachers who shaped your faith or the faith of others in your congregation?

b. How has disciple making happened in camp and Sunday school settings? In small groups and spiritual friendships? In other areas of church life?

c. How do your pastoral leaders function as disciplers in your congregation?

d. In what creative ways is the Christian story being told in your congregation?

e. How does your congregation practice ministries of reconciliation?

f. Which ongoing practices or customs of your congregation are important in shaping faith and calling people to growth? Which ones may be detrimental?

g. How do attitudes and practices regarding racism,

wealth, or other issues affect the discipling process in your congregation?

2. If you see the need to enhance and expand the discipling potential of the communal dimensions of congregational life, what needs to be changed? How will you begin to work at making these changes? Who can help your congregation make these changes?

For further reading and study:

The Hilarity of Community: Romans 12 and How to Be the Church by Marva J. Dawn. Eerdmans, 1992.

Community and Commitment by John Driver. Herald Press, 1976.

Becoming God's Community by John Driver. Mennonite Publishing House, 1981.

Community of Faith: Crafting Christian Communities Today by Evelyn Eaton Whitehead and James Whitehead. Twenty-Third Publications, 1992.

Chapter 5

How Do Formation and Transformation Occur in the Congregation's Life of Mission?

by G. Edwin Bontrager

In both the arenas of worship and the close-knit circle of communal life, faith is formed and shaped as Christians participate in the life of the church. Lives are transformed by the grace of God, in loving relationships, and through the active practice of ministry. A third essential arena of congregational life is found primarily beyond the walls of the church in the world. It is the arena of mission, the outwardly focused ministries of witness, service, and peacemaking. As Christians go about their daily lives in the world, their faith is also being formed and shaped by work and play, neighborhood involvement, relationships with others, and loving deeds.

Discipled by Personal Faith Sharing

Les told his pastor he didn't feel comfortable making contacts with congregational visitors in their homes with a presentation of the gospel. He had joined a 12-week class for personal faith sharing and then had gone out with the team responsible to follow up those who had visited the church worship service. However, he explained that since he had been exposed to the training and had helped to share faith in various homes, he himself was discipled as a witness. Now he found more courage to share his faith informally on the job and in the neighborhood. Sharing faith with others stimulated his own growth in faith.

Evangelism is sharing the good news of Christ and his kingdom. The Greek verb *Euanggelidzo,* which is used over fifty times in the New Testament, basically means "to proclaim the good news." But the noun form, *evangelist* is used only three times. By using verbs to describe evangelism, the Bible puts the emphasis on action.

Evangelism happens in many ways. For some people evangelism conjures images of a forced impersonal encounter with a religious fanatic; others visualize mass meetings in tents or stadiums. Still others see a charismatic preacher who uses sound waves to reach thousands of people at one time. Many have found belief in Christ and have joined communities of faith through these methods. But effective congregations do not rely on outsiders to do their evangelizing. They disciple their own members to become bearers of the good news.

Philemon 6 says, "I pray that you will be active in sharing your faith, so that you will have a full understanding of every good thing we have in Christ" (NIV). Some claim that to be an effective witness we first need to fully understand the doctrines of the Bible in full detail. They believe that in this way we can withstand every doubt or question a prospect would raise with us.

But discipling for personal witness happens best when Christians push out the edges of their witness comfort zone. Faltering steps coupled with prayer can evolve into a confident walk down the challenging pathway of witness. The expertise needed in piloting an airplane comes when the novice intentionally puts his hand on the stick. Then he carefully follows the steps that eventually allow him the freedom to take to the air alone. The best planned lesson prepared for a class on "How to Reach Your Neighbor for Christ" will be bereft of power if students fail to take action on their own level.

However, since not all congregational members possess the gift of evangelism, discipling will come through the use of other gifts. Some will engage in the role of witness simply by telling a friend their faith story. Peter challenged the Christians in Asia Minor, "Always be prepared to give an answer to everyone who asks you to give the reason for the hope that you have" (1 Peter 3:15, NIV). Churches in mission depend on people who are intercessors, as well as the mentors who walk alongside new Christians. They need leaders of discipling groups. Nurturing those new in faith results in the more knowledgeable and experienced Christian also being discipled.

Discipled by the Vitality of New Christians

Among long-term Christians, routine and tradition tend to produce tepid faith. Commitment to Christ is deeply anchored; loyalty to the people of God is without question. But where are the spontaneity and the outbursts of joy? Why do long-term Christians sometimes pull back from the call to ministry? Why must they be pressured to participate in the life of the church? Mature Christians are expected to be devoted and steadfast, but they often become serious, complacent, and comfortable.

New Christians, especially those who have found release from a tempestuous and shadowy past, often abound with exuberance and energy. Like the apostle Paul, the same personality that took them one direction and landed them into a colorful and reckless lifestyle now becomes touched with the Holy Spirit. They exude a creativity and passion that, when honed, directed, and nurtured, will enliven the church and set it on fire.

What a paradox exists in our congregations! Those who have been Christians for years are often bent under the weight of religion and the strain of church protocol. Yet those who are fresh in faith, enveloped with wonder and curiosity, energetically move ahead, pushing the boundaries of traditional expectations. If the church can hold the reins loosely and provide only the guidance that is necessary, there is no limit what can happen to a congregation infiltrated by new Christians. Those who have functioned as teachers and disciplers discover that they themselves are gaining new levels of maturity. Why? Because they are disciples under the tutelage of new Christians.

Questions about church structure or biblical doctrine might crop up: "Why does your church allow women to serve as leaders? Why do you put so much emphasis on Bible learning and internal growth? What are you doing to invite new people—non-Christians—to our church? You believe that one should not fight in the military, but why? We need to defend our country." These challenges, even rebukes, can send us back to the Scriptures and to an examination of our traditions. The old Christians can become even stronger in faith.

Discipled by Picking Up a Hammer and Trowel

"Service" has served Mennonites well when we think about our mission to people at home and abroad. Whether it's economic development overseas through Mennonite Central Committee (MCC), a Mennonite Disaster Service (MDS) stint in North America, or a Mennonite Economic Development Associate (MEDA) Project at home and overseas, many have been blessed while sharing a blessing. But how can such service and justice ministries disciple us, help us grow in faith, and bring Christian faith to others?

Intergenerational teams are one arena for discipling. Because youth and adults often go their separate ways in society and the church, they seldom become acquainted. The natural opportunities for sharing faith between the generations may be few and far between. But when young and old rub shoulders on a work project, they form relationships in which faith sharing can occur.

The old may be astounded at the depth of conviction among young people; youth may be just as startled to discover how adults struggle to grow in their faith. The faith of both groups is challenged and strengthened by the other—another building block in making disciples. Furthermore, when young and old Christians work together because of the love of Jesus for people they don't know, they lift a banner of hope for those without faith.

Another arena for discipling is service teams that include the unchurched. What about inviting non-Christians to join us when we work on a Habitat for Humanity project in our neighborhood? How might this action build a stronger church? People who have not yet claimed Jesus as Lord have skills and experience they are willing to share in altruistic ways. Inviting them to serve will not only allow them to build a better humanity, but will return to them inner satisfaction and fulfillment. Such an experience may be just what they need to lead them a step closer to Christ and the community of faith. Beyond that, we in turn discover inner spiritual strength as we minister side by side with people who, though they are not yet Christian, we care deeply about.

So what are the benefits for Christians who take the time to pick up their shovels and dig out mud after a flood? Or use their scrub brushes to clean toilets? Or wield their tools to repair a house? Winona Houser, a teen who joined a service team, exclaimed, "Four days [of service] has given me sore fingers from hours of guitar playing, a stiff neck from painting, a bunch of great new friends, and a heart that is more willing to listen to God" (Harrisburg Minicourse Gives New Friends and Learning," *Lancaster Conference*

News, July 28, 1996).

The discipling potential of service ministries is legendary. In serving others we learn compassion and mercy. We discover that thankfulness is not only a product of idyllic surroundings. When Christians become acquainted with sorrow and loss and the offensive or vile side of life, their hearts are softened. The compassion ratio grows higher and higher. A big step toward Christian maturity is to see human need through the eyes of Jesus.

Discipled by Peacemaking

Christ is the embodiment of peace. Reconciliation between individuals in families, gangs on the street, and fractured groups within the church displays the love of Jesus to its fullest. New members are attracted to a church that is at peace within itself. The congregation that makes a good impression upon seekers is one that works for peace and justice where there is violence and poverty. Two examples of how churches have integrated peace and evangelism are Belmont Mennonite Church, Elkhart, Indiana; and Calvary Community Church in Hampton, Virginia.

Belmont

A few years ago in the Elkhart community, a 19-year-old young man was killed by a gun that was in the illegal possession of a 15-year-old. Duane Beck, pastor of the Belmont congregation, was invited to say a few words and offer a prayer at the funeral. It was then that he said, "If Trevor's death is not to be in vain, we need to do something positive. We need to get guns out of kids' hands. If you take the initiative," he told the kids, "I'll help you. You know people with guns. I know people with money."

As a result of the challenge, 69 guns from 55 people were collected, and $2,000 was given in return. One does not know how many more injuries and deaths were prevented by this one feat. Beck said, "Working to stop gun violence is an evangelization and mission issue because it's about being salt and light in the city. It's about peace and justice. Often we think of peace and justice in terms of issues rather than people. But this involved families and young people grieving, so it was a pastoral care issue."

Calvary

The Calvary Community Church in Hampton, Virginia, is one of the fastest growing Mennonite churches in North America. Along with a strong evangelistic outreach program, it works with many justice issues in its African-American community.

Annually the Calvary congregation sponsors a Community Unity Day. The purpose of this Saturday event is to bridge the gap from the church to the surrounding community. People may be suspicious of the church. "It's just out to get you to come in and support their program and give money" is the accusation sometimes heard. So Calvary shares a wholistic concept of the church.

The day includes a financial counseling booth along with educational counseling. Direction is given on how to prepare for GED tests, as well as how to move toward college or vocational programs. Other booths focus on building self-esteem, how-to-find-a-job interviews, health fitness guidance, and information for purchasing a home. Medical personnel do blood and cholesterol screening. While the adults are involved in these activities, the children are entertained by puppets and a carnival.

A lot of personal discipling results from these projects at both Belmont and Calvary. People are able to get in touch with their own feelings about those who are victimized by violence and poverty. Personal bridges are built between church members and those who suffer. Peacemaking, working to erase poverty, and evangelization are inseparable parts of the mission of the church.

Discipled by Inviting Others
to Come Along to Church

Martin Marty, a Lutheran church historian, said that "the word *invite* defines the difference between churches that grow and those that do not." Though more than half of the unchurched in North America are not opposed to being part of a church community someday, we can be sure of this fact—they will not attend unless they are invited. Ads in the paper may help, the "Welcome" sign out front is nice, but the attraction comes most through a personal invitation.

A research questionnaire used for the Living In Faithful Evangelism (LIFE) project in many Mennonite churches included a question about how often church members invite someone to church. The score on that question was almost always lower than any other. Why? Congregational members have not been encouraged by their leaders to invite people. Pastors may not see inviting as an integral feature of discipleship within the congregation. Reading the Bible, praying, ethical living, and attending church are all stressed as ingredients of the Christian walk. However, bringing people along to church is often forgotten as a key component of Christian maturity.

When congregational members freely extend invitations to their co-workers and neighbors, they will receive some positive responses, but they may also be faced with excuses, questions, and downright refusal. After a while church members might say, "It's not worth it. I really am feeling rejected, as though what I believe is not very important. Furthermore, I'm faced with questions I can't answer, and that's embarrassing."

However, if we examine these responses and look at them positively, we might exclaim, "What a chance for Christian growth!" Certainly rejection is a reaction no one would choose, but when it is faced and an appropriate response is made, this is a chance for personal growth. It might cause one to have stronger reason to flee to the church community for repose and renewal, but one can then emerge more stalwart and solid.

People will ask questions: "I've heard of Mennonites before. What does your church believe?" "Do you offer anything for people who have just gone through a divorce?" "I always need to work at the hospital on Sunday mornings. Do you have Saturday night services?" "I've thought about going to church, but I'm not sure it's worth it. Why do you go?" At first some inquiries may stymie the inviter, but they provide a framework for further study and personal growth. Other questions may suggest strategic planning in congregational life such as the need for support groups or alternate worship services to reach people more effectively.

Inviting people to church rarely brings reproach unless the inviter becomes angry at the one who spurns the invitation! Usually extending that invitation brings personal growth as well as congregational growth.

Discipled by Expanding Our Circle of Friends

Welcoming non-Christian friends into our homes will also shape us further for mission. Sharing common problems of life makes us real and vulnerable. Others can see that we are not the stereotypically perfect Christian family or individual down the street. Such honesty allows others, who seek shelter from the storms of life, to probe and test the genuineness of our faith. Although some Christians panic and cower in fear when they think of this kind of encounter, these interchanges often drive us to Scripture for help and paint for us a new picture of the grace of God. Our willingness to be Christ's disciples day in and day out on our own street can be a means of personal spiritual growth as well as an invitation to growth to our neighbors.

Congregational Checkup

In your leadership team or discussion group, consider the following questions:

1. How have you experienced mission as a setting for formation and transformation in your congregation? What stories can you tell of witness, service or peacemaking that changed or renewed you or others in your church?

2. If you would like to enhance and expand the discipling potential of the mission life of your congregation, what changes must be made? How would you begin to work at making these changes? Who can help your church make such changes?

Putting the Arenas Back Together Again

While we have taken congregational life apart and examined how each arena becomes a context for discipling, we must recognize again that the three arenas are not truly distinct from each other. Even as the congregation is engaged in worship, relationships are being nourished in the community of faith and a vision for witness and service is being proclaimed. As the church goes about being a family, it engages in prayer and reaches beyond its own boundaries to love and serve the world. The congregation's life of ministry in the world includes prayer and worship and is dependent upon healthy relationships within the body. As all three arenas interrelate and function cooperatively, both individuals and the church grow in love of God, self, and neighbor.

In every arena of congregational life—whether in the community at worship, in relationships with each other, or in ministries of witness and service—Christians are becoming disciples of Christ. The lifelong process of becoming like Christ and living as Christ's followers in the world is both a purpose and a by-product of congregational life. Thus we cannot say that a congregation has a disci-

pling ministry; instead we recognize that congregational life itself is a discipling ministry.

All that we are and do as God's people has the potential to deepen, weaken, or destroy our faith. The ability of the church to fulfill the call of Jesus to make disciples depends on the spiritual vitality and quality of the congregation's common life. Fulfilling the call of Jesus to make disciples also depends, however, on another ingredient of congregational life. In the next chapter (6), we examine this new ingredient and demonstrate how it relates to the three essential, interdependent arenas of worship, community, and mission.

Congregational Checkup

In your leadership team or discussion group, take time to put the church back together and see it as a whole organism.

1. How do you see communal relationships and a call to mission being nurtured and strengthened in worship?

2. How do you see attentiveness to God's presence and the practice of worship being encouraged in community life? How is the church's mission kept in focus as the congregation nurtures a healthy sense of family and accountability?

3. How is the congregation depending on the Spirit as it engages in mission? Is prayer an integral part of mission? Are relationships within the body of Christ strengthened as people participate in witness, service, and peacemaking?

4. If there is a lack of integration among the three arenas, what needs to be changed? How will you begin to work at making these changes? Who can help you make such changes?

For further reading and study:

Widening the Welcome of Your Church by Fred Bernhard and Steve Clapp. LifeQuest, 1996. Available from The Andrew Center, 1451 Dundee Ave., Elgin, IL 60120. Telephone: 1 800 774-3360. Study guide available.

Following in the Footsteps of Paul by G. Edwin Bontrager. Mennonite Publishing House, 1994. Interactive video, student and leader's guide available.

Sharing Living Water by Steve Clapp and Sam Detweiler. LifeQuest, 1996. Available from The Andrew Center. Study guide available.

The Purpose-Driven Church by Rick Warren. Zondervan, 1995.

Welcome! A Biblical and Practical Guide to Receiving New Members by Ervin R. Stutzman. Herald Press, 1990.

Chapter 6

Discipling for Worship, Community and Mission

by Marlene Kropf and Carlos Romero

In chapter 1, the church's task of making disciples was described as two-fold:

First, To call people to faith and baptize them in the name of the triune God;

Second, To teach them to observe all things that Jesus commanded—to love God, self, and neighbor—and come to mature faith.

In chapters 2, 3, 4 and 5, each arena of congregational life was examined to discover the inner workings of the discipling process as the church goes about its day-to-day ministries.

*In the arena of **worship**, seekers and believers are formed and shaped in their faith as they see a vision of who God is and hear the call to become followers of Christ. In the arena of **community** life, members are formed and transformed in their faith through relationships and ministries within the body of Christ. In the arena of **mission**, people grow as they act on their faith as witnesses, servants, and peacemakers in the world.*

Making disciples is a by-product of each arena of congregational life.

Not Another Arena But a Process

However, disciple making is more than a by-product. While not an arena in itself, disciple making is an intentional and focused process of instruction and training which circulates continuously and vigorously throughout all the arenas. It equips people for participation in the three arenas of congregational life. The overall purposes of this intentional mode of discipling are threefold:

First, to enable for worship for the sake of creating a faithful covenant community who know and love God;

Second, to equip for community for the sake of transformation into Christlikeness;

Third, to empower for mission for the sake of carrying out God's loving purposes in the world through the power of the Spirit.

The trinitarian character and structure which undergird the Congregational Discipling Vision is an intentional framework. Just as a theological understanding of God-as-Trinity (three-in-one) reflects the fullness of God, so a trinitarian framework for understanding the church represents the fullness of God's life expressed in the congregation.

Worship is the arena in which Christians receive their identity and express their commitment to being God's covenant people (1 Peter 2:9).

Life in **community** is the arena in which the church functions as the body of Christ—a living organism incarnating the love of Christ and sharing life in unity (1 Corinthians 12:27).

In the third arena, **mission**, the church is envisioned as the dwelling of the Spirit—a dynamic, discerning, gifted witness of God's love and power in the world (Ephesians 2:22).

A Reciprocal Process

Diagram B

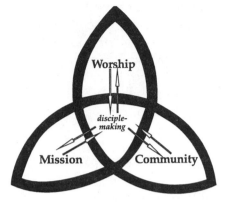

As illustrated by two-way arrows in diagram B, a reciprocal relationship always exists between the discipling process and each dimension of congregational life.

First, people are discipled *for* their participation in worship, community, and mission.

Second, people are also discipled *by* their participation in each arena of congregational life.

For example, one's faith in God is strengthened by singing meaningful hymns in the worship service; but one's participation in worship through singing is enhanced if the rudiments of music are known— how to follow simple musical markings, how to cooperate with other voices, or how to read the information printed on the page about the authorship of the hymn. Knowing that a hymn is a thousand years old and has been sung by Christians throughout the centuries adds new layers of meaning. In the same way, a worshiper's faith in God is often challenged by effective public reading of Scripture; those who read Scripture, however, benefit from training to carry out this ministry more effectively.

When leaders speak of the discipling process, it must always be seen as a two-directional process. One direction focuses on the arenas. It asks the leaders to attend to the discipling process as it occurs within each arena. The other direction focuses on the process of discipling. It asks the church's instructional and training ministries to equip people for active and fruitful ministry in the church and in the world.

Christian Education as Discipling

If you were a congregational leader seeking to strengthen the discipling processes in your church, where would you turn? One important place to turn is to the congregation's educational ministries. Although you could also consider the roles of parents, mentors, or pastors, a natural place to begin in the gathered community is with teachers and educational leaders.

Christian education occurs in many contexts such as families, camps, small groups, retreats, clubs, Bible school, special events, and conferences. On a week-to-week basis, however, congregations rely on the Sunday school to carry an important piece of the Congregational Discipling Vision. Because of this, congregations need to make careful decisions about the curriculum they choose to use. Do the materials reflect Anabaptist theology? Will they shape faith in ways that support the congregation's discipling vision? Will they support the denomination's long-range goals embodied in its statement "Vision: Healing and Hope"?

If the congregation is using denominational curriculum products such as Jubilee: God's Good News, The LINK Youth Bible Studies, Generation Why Bible Studies, or the Adult Bible Study, they can be confident that the material reflects the Congregational Discipling Vision and the denominational vision. Curriculum writers have been carefully trained to express the Congregational Discipling Vision and to prepare lesson guides that form and shape faith in ways that are compatible with the church's commitments.

As congregational leaders examine all the possible settings for discipling, they may want to ask," What essential knowledge, attitudes, and skills need to be cultivated so growth toward mature faith occurs?"

In the arena of **worship**, for example, "What knowledge, attitudes, and skills are needed for effective participation?" "How do worshipers meet God?" "Do people know how to pray?" "Do they understand basic Christian symbols?" "Do they understand the purpose of preaching?"

In the arena of **community**, "Do people know how to listen to each other?" "Are they equipped to engage in and resolve conflict?" "Do they know how to share their life in Christ with each other?"

In the **mission** arena, "Does the congregation have a strategy for welcoming new members?" "Is an information package and follow-up available for visitors?" "Are greeters trained for their ministry of hospitality?" "Do members know how to share their faith in simple, effective ways?"

The charts of the three arenas, see pages 54-56, propose a sample list of questions to guide educational leaders as they design the congregational discipling processes. You may wish to add additional questions to address the unique situation of your congregation.

Chart 1
Discipling for Worship

To participate fully in worship and realize its potential for faith formation, worshipers need instruction and training for worship. The following sample questions are suggested to guide leaders as they design a discipling process and prepare appropriate curricular strategies to form people for their life as worshipers.

How can educational ministries enable for worship?

1. How can education help worshipers become aware of God's presence? How can people discover a whole range of biblical images of God from the most majestic and powerful to the most tender and compassionate? How can people learn to open themselves to God's love and guidance?

2. How can education encourage people to claim the biblical story and biblical faith for their own lives?

3. How can education lead people to understand the history and practices of Jewish and Christian-Mennonite worship?

4. How can education enable people to experience the power of story, ritual, symbol, and music?

5. How can education guide people to engage in personal spiritual disciplines or learn a variety of ways to pray?

6. How can education prepare people for joyful participation in giving offerings?

7. How can education equip people with skills for worship leading and participation?

8. How can education train people to practice hospitality to newcomers who join them in worship?

9.

Chart 2
Discipling for Community

To participate fully in the life of community and realize its potential for faith formation, members need instruction and training for communal life. The following sample questions are suggested to guide leaders as they design a discipling process and prepare appropriate curricular strategies to form people for their life in community.

How can educational ministries prepare members to live in community?

1. How can education help people become aware of self in God's presence and receive God's healing love and forgiving grace?

2. How can education encourage people to embrace the biblical story and the historical traditions of the church?

3. How can education equip people with interpersonal skills such as listening and communicating effectively?

4. How can education prepare couples for marriage? How can it nurture their ongoing relationship?

5. How can education develop aptitudes for discipling, giving spiritual direction, counseling, parenting, teaching, mentoring, and leading small groups?

6. How can education train people to participate effectively in conflict mediation or resolution?

7. How can education cultivate respect for people of all races, cultures, and economic groups?

8. How can education nurture the practice of hospitality and generous sharing with others in the community of faith?

9.

Chart 3
Discipling for Mission

To participate fully in the congregation's life of mission and realize its potential for faith formation, those engaged in mission need instruction and training for the tasks of mission. The following sample questions are suggested to guide leaders as they design a discipling process and prepare appropriate curricular strategies to form people for their life in mission.

How can educational ministries empower for mission?

1. How can education help people learn to discern the voice of God and recognize God's activity in the world?

2. How can education encourage people to receive and share the good news of the gospel and God's loving invitation to all?

3. How can education enable people to identify and claim gifts for ministry?

4. How can education develop multicultural awareness and sensitivity to the uniqueness of persons and communities?

5. How can education call people to join the struggle against violence, oppression, economic injustice, and racism?

6. How can education awaken people to their responsibility to care for God's created world?

7. How can education foster cheerful and sacrificial giving to those in need?

8. How can education equip people to befriend and serve the poor, weak, and disabled?

9.

10.

Two Goals for Discipling: Integration and Intentionality

Sometimes educational ministries become detached from the larger vision and goals of the congregation. Because these ministries often have their own organization and administration, they may not be closely linked to the three primary arenas of congregational life: worship, community, and mission. In such situations, the congregation may suffer from competing purposes. Conflicts can arise. Leaders may burn out out as they try to juggle too many priorities. The greatest loss is that the discipling process is weakened because of lack of integration.

In a time when the church faces great competition from secular values and priorities, it cannot afford to waste resources or lose the effectiveness of each setting for discipling. Careful thinking and creative planning are required to maximize the potential of each context and insure that all efforts support a common vision. What might such intentional, integrated planning look like?

One model of integrated planning is for congregations to choose a yearly theme which expresses a particular dimension of the larger vision. When this theme has been discerned and adopted, each leadership group makes plans for the year which support and develop some aspect of the annual theme.

For example, in one congregation, the pastor and lay leaders chose the year-long theme "To Know Christ and to Make Christ Known." When worship and educational leaders implemented the theme, they emphasized the first part of the theme, "To Know Christ," during the first half of the year. They selected the Gospel of Mark as the study focus for adults as well as for preaching. In addition, an adult Sunday school class was offered on spiritual disciplines and focused on praying the Scriptures.

During the second half of the year, the emphasis shifted to "Making Christ Known." The congregation engaged in an exercise of gift discernment and then participated in adult classes which emphasized skill development for witness and service. In further support of the theme, a class was offered in friendship evangelism and another in the ministry of hospitality.

Another example of an integrated focus occurred when the new *Confession of Faith in a Mennonite Perspective* was being tested in 1994-1995. Many churches chose to focus on one article per week in worship and offered discussion settings for adults and youth during Sunday school. Other congregations regularly integrate the themes of Sunday morning by using the Revised Common Lectionary Scripture texts, Uniform Series texts, or Jubilee: God's Good News texts (children's curriculum) as a biblical focus for both worship and education. The summer quarter of Jubilee provides materials for integrating all ages on Sunday morning around common biblical themes.

Story from Normal, Illinois

When the Congregational Discipling Vision was being tested in congregations, the **Mennonite Church of Normal** (Illinois) engaged in a creative, experimental series called "Journey With Jesus." Their focus included both church structure and thematic integration during the seasons from Advent to Easter. During their experiment, Sunday morning was divided into three segments: worship, learning experiences, and closing assembly.

When worshipers arrived each week, they stopped at the customs booth in the church foyer, got their passports stamped with the day's location, and received their tour program (church bulletins). In the entry area, a large banner with red letters proclaimed the destination for the day: Bethlehem, the Jordan River, Cana, the Sea of Galilee, Capernaum, Jerusalem, and so on. A large poster in the entry also kept the congregation informed of progress on a Habitat for Humanity house which they helped to build during this series. This project was chosen because Jesus was a carpenter; building a house would be a good way to identify with the life of Jesus.

Worship experiences included singing, prayer, Scripture reading, input (sermon, slide show, dialogue, etc.), and an anthem by the choir. During the learning experiences, people of all ages chose from many options to reflect on the story and theme for the day and to respond to it: storytelling, video, drama, learning games, Bible study, discussion groups, or memory drills. During the final assembly, people shared from their learning experiences or their living during the week. Mission opportunities or memory challenges were presented, followed by a prayer of blessing for the week to come.

The project team who guided the series was amazed at the willingness of the congregation to accept assignments during the experiment. A greater number of people than usual were involved as leaders each week, yet the team had no difficulty finding people to serve. The congregation also demonstrated considerable openness to innovations in both worship and education. People affirmed the opportunity to expand their relationships in the congregation across the generations.

Story from Toronto, Ontario

A congregational decision on building a church facility to make room for expanding ministries was the context of a Congregational Discipling Vision experiment at the **Danforth Morningside Mennonite Church** in inner-city Toronto, Ontario. Their project team led a congregational planning process that resulted in an integrated strategy for worship, community life, and the church's mission in their area. Called "Upon This Rock," the purpose of the experiment was to help the congregation reexamine its own identity, explore a biblical theology of building, and mobilize for rebuilding the church in the future.

Included in the strategy was as a two-hour Sunday morning block of time in which all ages engaged in Bible study: an exploration of Israel's struggle for faith identity found in the Old Testament stories of exodus and exile, and the New Testament texts focusing on the church as a body.

A guest storyteller came one weekend to show slides and tell the Anabaptist story—another piece of the congregation's identity. A large poster was painted showing the biblical, historical, and cultural roots of this congregation. Other community-building events included the Art and Talent Show as well as the Heritage Night one Saturday featuring games, storytelling, and old family photographs. A Sunday afternoon event called a "Menno Alley Rally" focused on the surrounding community where the congregation carried out its mission. As they took a walking tour, members of the congregation became better acquainted with the history and people of the neighborhood that surrounded their meetinghouse. The integrated experiences in worship, community, and mission provided a foundation for the decision the congregation needed to make about a new facility.

Many more stories could be told of the creative ways congregations have undergirded and revitalized the discipling purposes of the church. Such intentional and integrated planning happens best if congregational structures support and facilitate cooperative discernment and planning. Chapter 15 will pick up this theme and expand it further.

The fruitfulness of the discipling process ultimately depends on the Holy Spirit's work in the lives of individuals and communities of faith. Congregational leaders can cooperate with the Spirit's work by being attentive to sparks of interest and thoughtful questions. They can also cooperate with the Spirit by intentionally planning a well-rounded, integrated educational program that supports the common focus of all the discipling ministries. When prior-

ities are clear, leaders will have energy and vision for their call, and the people of God will be strengthened in their quest to love God, self, and neighbor with their whole heart, soul, and mind.

Congregational Checkup

In your leadership team or discussion group, consider the following questions:

1. Describe how the educational ministry of your congregation supports the discipling potential of the arenas of worship, community, and mission. Using all the education settings of the past year, review the ways each one contributed to formation for worship, community, and mission.

2. Use the three charts earlier in this chapter to name the specific goals for disciple making in your congregation. Do the suggested goals fit your congregation and your vision? What goals would you add?

3. How intentional and integrated are the discipling ministries of your congregation? Do leaders sometimes struggle from overwork or burnout? Do members sometimes feel that too many things are going on at once? Do leaders of the various arenas occasionally find themselves in conflict with each other? If you experience fragmentation, what can be done to bring the parts of the whole back together again?

4. List all of the standing committees in your church. In what ways does each one contribute to the worship, community, and mission aspects of the congregation? In what way does each committee serve an educational function for its members and the congregation? Make a circle for each committee. In pie chart fashion, show how each one is

involved in each of the three arenas as follows:

Diagram B-1

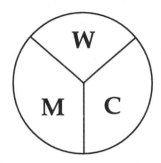

What surprised you? What changes are needed?

For further reading and study:
Fashion Me A People: Curriculum in the Church by Maria Harris. Westminster/John Knox, 1989.

Educating Congregations: The Future of Christian Education by Charles R. Foster. Abingdon Press 1994.

Christian Spiritual Formation in the Church and Classroom by Susanne Johnson. Abingdon Press, 1989.

To Know As We Are Known: A Spirituality of Education by Parker J. Palmer. Harper & Row, 1983.

Chapter 7

Jesus as Model Discipler

by Daniel Schipani

A primary biblical foundation for the Congregational Discipling Vision is the great commandment. This text reveals the purpose or desired outcome of all the discipling ministries of the church: to enable people to love God, self, and neighbor with their whole heart, soul, mind, and strength (Mark 12:29-31).

Another gospel text sheds light on the question of how such formation and transformation occur. The story of the walk to Emmaus (Luke 24:13-35) portrays the risen Christ as discipler. In this account we discover key principles for effective discipling.

The Disciples

The two disciples seem to be common folk—they were not two of the twelve. They are leaving Jerusalem, like so many others, on the Sunday after Passover. They carry a sense of defeat; they are confused, baffled by doubt, fear, and anxiety. Disillusionment mingles with some hope because of the word they had received from "some women of our group (v. 22)." But they have many questions.

The disciples need a new sense of direction. This struggle for some kind of resolution is an essential attitude for transformation—i.e., education—to take place. To want more light and to want to grow is crucial indeed.

This desire motivates these disciples to welcome the

"stranger" and to discuss the Scriptures with him. Thus the first step of community building takes place: they readily share their stories and visions.

This is our *first* insight into Christian education: for education to take place, we don't need teachers but disciples. We need people willing to become eager followers of Jesus. In fact, one of the wisest attitudes we may have and one of the more meaningful prayers we may pray is, simply, "God, teach me. I need to know. I really want to learn and grow." Good teachers, like Jesus, will in turn elicit and reinforce that kind of disposition.

A *second* insight soon becomes apparent. In the walk along the road to Emmaus, an event takes place which becomes the turning point of the story: the disciples put their faith into action by inviting the stranger to share a meal with them. Thus the second phase of community building occurs. By receiving the gift of hospitality, the stranger becomes their "companion"—a word derived from the Latin *cum panis*, "with bread."

We need reflection and action, understanding as well as practice. Reaching out to the stranger is indeed a major dimension of the gospel of the reign of God. And community building is a central concern in the educational ministry of the church.

The disciples on the road to Emmaus give us a *third* important insight into Christian education. After their moment of understanding around the table, when they seem to be making sense of the whole thing—the meaning of hope in Christ, the true way of redemption or liberation, the acknowledgment of the actual presence of the risen Lord—they decide to go back to Jerusalem. There is where the action is, the action must continue. They must go and tell what has happened. The road to Emmaus does not only lead to Emmaus; it goes back to Jerusalem as well.

The Teacher

We now turn to the "stranger"—who is Jesus himself. Again, at least three new clues about the nature of Christian education are illustrated.

First, we observe that this teacher (Jesus) joins the disciples right where they are in the journey, entering their reality. Jesus does not tell them who he is. He does not dictate the truth of the Scripture and the gospel in a paternalistic or authoritarian fashion. Instead, he encourages them to share their story—memories as well as dreams—so as to become actively and personally involved in the discipling process.

Second, Jesus does much more than listen. He summarizes their story in a way that captures their imagination. This opens their hearts to hear another view of the events which had happened. Jesus also provides needed resources for a new understanding of salvation in light of the biblical story. This enables the disciples to relate this new understanding to their own pilgrimage and their own hope. Their human journey is becoming a sacred journey as well.

Third, we observe that the teaching methods Jesus uses include a variety of activities. He certainly engages in much more than cognitive and verbal transactions. His tutelage is also richer than mere instruction because he teaches with a spirit of compassion and solidarity, in a climate of fellowship and companionship.

Indeed, Jesus accepts the gift of hospitality, puts himself at the disposal of the disciples, and serves them in their own setting. Eventually he leaves the scene at the opportune moment—something that many educators have a hard time doing!

Context and Timing

As we study the story of Emmaus from an educational perspective, we realize that learning and transformation take place in different surroundings: Jerusalem, the road,

Emmaus. We too are invited to engage in discipling—to educate and be educated—in changing locations and at opportune times.

We often favor planned instruction and guided learning in our educational program. Yet these settings can be more or less formal and casual. There is so much to learn in the very experience of fellowship and communion, in and through worship and celebration, in the proclamation by words and deeds, or in mutual discipling. This rich, multi-faceted context of Christian education brings our attention to teachable moments in our own environments: home, congregation, neighborhood, school, work—and even on the road.

Process and Content

In the teaching ministry of the church, how we learn and what we learn are inseparable. This intimate relationship is well illustrated in the Emmaus story.

The passage depicts a variety of themes around the central motif of the way of the cross and resurrection. A rich and complex agenda becomes the subject matter: current events are discussed; people's fears, hopes, and actions are considered; personal feelings and thoughts are shared, the Scriptures are searched anew. This is a very inclusive curriculum indeed.

It confirms that God is interested in anything and everything that is relevant for us—and that God's Spirit desires to lead us in the midst of our quests for truth and understanding! What a wonderful model! What a responsibility this places on Christian educators!

Another quick look at the resurrected Jesus as teacher points to a variety of methods he employed: use of questions, discussion reflection, dialogical and critical interpretation, exposition of the Word, dramatization. Learning is rich and profound because several dimensions of the disciples' character have been engaged. Their minds, their hearts and their wills have been transformed.

Purpose

What is the goal of the educational journey in the congregation? It is certainly more than physically recognizing Jesus. It is more more than merely knowing the Bible. The purpose is to be formed, transformed, and empowered with the gospel of the reign of God. In fact, this reflection on the Emmaus story helps us to affirm the central role of education in the life of the church. The purpose is three-fold:

First, the discipling journey aims to foster and enhance worship; learning and adoration are linked. Genuine worship involves and invites future learning. Educational ministry can in turn lead to more meaningful worship. Education for faith and discipleship enables worship.

Second, the discipling journey is to promote and facilitate the nurturing of faith in the context of community formation and development. The two disciples return to share their testimony with others. In turn, a growing faith and a maturing community will call and make space for a sound educational ministry. Education for faith and discipleship equips for community.

Third, faithful witness as proclamation and service is clearly a direct result of the encounter with the risen Christ, the liberating teacher of this narrative. To the extent that Christian education is true to its nature and role, mission is also enhanced and revitalized. Education for faith and discipleship empowers for mission.

As in the case of worship and community, mission work enriches the educational ministry. As we engage in mission, we will always meet other strangers. With them, we will always encounter the living Christ again and again!

Congregational Checkup
With your leadership team or discussion group, consider the following questions:

1. What does the story of two disciples who met the risen Christ on the road to Emmaus reveal about Jesus as a teacher? How does it illuminate what is important in the teaching-learning process?

2. How does your congregation train teachers? Mentors? Other leaders? Spiritual guides? How can these leaders be equipped to more fully follow the model of Jesus as they guide others in their growth to mature faith?

For further reading and study:
Christian Religious Education: Sharing Our Story and Vision by Thomas H. Groome. Harper & Row, 1980.

Chapter 8

Envisioning the Future

by Abe Bergen

Vision, Priorities, and Strategies

"Where there is no vision, the people perish" (Proverbs 29:18, KJV) expresses the importance of having a vision for group or institutional identity. A vision empowers by providing incentive for action. Without a vision, one loses focus, direction, and motivation. A common vision unifies, provides clarity of purpose, and describes the quality of life aspired to by the group.

A denominational vision reflects its deepest values based on its understanding of the Scriptures. Like the pillar of fire that guided the Israelites in the desert, a vision is a light in the distance that points the way a denomination is headed. Such a vision can channel the people's energy and renew congregational ministries and structures.

Creating a denominational vision is hard work and requires careful discernment. For congregations to accept a denominational vision or to create their own vision also requires effort. Every congregation is challenged to be proactive in claiming a vision and thinking through the implications of that vision for its life together.

Since a vision statement expresses the core values of a denomination, it gives rise to priorities and strategies. Priorities are the emphases that are needed at a particular time in the life of the church. Each priority is based on a perceived need that has been identified as a concern.

Giving attention to these priorities will bring members closer to the quality of life expressed in the vision.

Strategies, sometimes called goals, are the means to get to the desired ends. These are the specific actions of congregations that begin to make priorities a reality. Strategies must be specific and measurable so progress can be assessed. They enable the implementation of a vision through workable actions. A time comes when a denomination or congregation will reevaluate its vision based on a new self-understanding or a renewed sense of what God is calling them to become. Such rethinking may give rise to a new vision with subsequently new priorities and strategies.

Diagram C

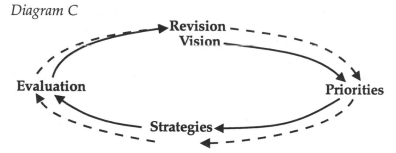

Vision: Healing and Hope

Beginning in 1991, leaders from the Mennonite Church and the General Conference Mennonite Church began meeting to discern a new vision for these two denominations. For several years they prayed, read widely, and reflected on the pain that was evident in the church and the world. They consulted leaders throughout both denominations in an effort to discern where God was leading them. In time, they believed God was guiding them to the following statement of vision:

God calls us to be followers of Jesus Christ and, by the power of the Holy Spirit, to grow as communities of grace, joy, and peace, so that God's healing and hope flow through us to the world.

This statement called, "Vision: Healing and Hope" is an effort to discern God's call to these Mennonite bodies on the eve of the twenty-first century. It points a direction that might be taken in the coming decade or decades. This statement is rooted in the belief that any vision for these Mennonite bodies needs to be based on the life and teachings of Jesus and must reflect the historic calling of the church to peacemaking and discipleship.

Vision: Healing and Hope sets forth three main callings:

First, a call to a renewed commitment and a deeper relationship with Jesus Christ.

Second, a call to allow the Spirit of God to transform our churches so members can experience God's healing and hope in their lives.

Third, a call to allow God's love to bring healing and hope to a broken world through our lives.

Rooted in biblical teaching and affirming the historic calling of Mennonites, Vision: Healing and Hope gives rise to new priorities based on perceived needs within the church and the world. The subsequent priorities are an attempt to respond redemptively to the brokenness and pain being experienced in the church and beyond. This vision and accompanying priorities were affirmed by the Mennonite Church and the General Conference Mennonite Church in their respective delegate sessions in July 1995.

Vision: Healing and Hope addresses priorities in the same three arenas that have been addressed by the Congregational Discipling Vision—the arenas of worship, community, and mission. The difference is that Vision: Healing and Hope provides specific content for what will be developed in the various arenas of congregational life.

The relationship of Congregational Discipling to Vision: Healing and Hope can be diagrammed as follows:

Diagram D

Spirituality: Enrich our prayer, worship, and study of the scriptures.

Stewardship: Offer all that we are and have to God.

Evangelism: Invite others to faith in Jesus Christ.

Peace and Reconciliation: Seek God's peace in our homes, work, neighborhoods and the world.

Leadership: Call and nurture congregational leaders for ministry in a changing environment.

Community: Practice love, forgiveness and hospitality that affirms our diversity and heals our brokenness.

God calls us to be followers of Jesus Christ and,
by the power of the Holy Spirit,
to grow as communities of grace, joy, and peace,
so that God's healing and hope flow
through us to the world.

Discerning Priorities and Developing Strategies

The creators of Vision: Healing and Hope have identified six priorities for the church that are related to the three arenas of the Congregational Discipling Vision. Some congregations are already working at one or more of these priorities as illustrated in chart 4 and the stories that follow. It is hoped that congregations will continue to give attention to those priorities which represent their strengths while simultaneously working at those areas where they are weak.

Chart 4

Congregational Discipling	Vision H&H Priorities	Congregational Examples
Worship: The way we relate to God.	1. Enrich our prayer, worship, and study of the scriptures. 2. Offer all that we are and have to God.	1. Bethel Mennonite Ch., Winnipeg, Manitoba 2. Kern Road Mennonite Ch., South Bend, Indiana
Community: The way we relate to the people of God.	3. Call and nurture congregational leaders for ministry in a changing environment. 4. Practice love, forgiveness and hospitality that affirms our diversity and heals our brokenness..	3. St Jacobs Mennonite Ch., St Jacobs, Ontario 4. Comunidad de Fe Mennonite Ch., Chicago, Illinois
Mission: The way we relate to the world.	5. Invite others to faith in Jesus Christ. 6. Seek God's peace in our homes, work, neighborhood and the world.	5. Wellspring Christian Fellowship, Clearbrook, British Columbia 6. Church Without Wall, Elkhart, Indiana

Worship: Priorities about how we come to follow Jesus Christ more faithfully

1. To enrich our prayer, worship, and study of the Scriptures.

Faithful followers of Jesus Christ want their relationship with Christ to grow. In an increasingly individualistic, affluent society, we face constant temptation to become self-reliant, to assume that we do not need God, that we can solve our own problems, and that possessions will take care of our needs. Spiritual disciplines open our hearts and shape our thoughts in ways that open us to the teachings of Christ and allow our lives to reflect greater faithfulness to Christ.

Bethel Mennonite Church, Winnipeg, Manitoba, began an ecumenically based Bible study program in 1989 called "Bethel Bible Series." After a two-week orientation for associate pastor Dave Bergen, five teacher candidates were recruited to begin a two-year study program. They met up to three hours every week for two years. The study program took them through the entire Bible and included homework assignments and tests.

After the training program was completed, these newly trained teachers recruited students and took them through the Bible in a less rigorous, though still comprehensive, program. The two years of study were divided into six units of seven sessions each. These units were offered by the five teachers on a staggered basis so if students needed to drop out for a unit, they could join another group at a later time and continue where they left off. One goal of the study series was for participants to read the entire Bible in the course of two years. Six years later about 120 people have completed the study program.

2. To offer all we are and have to God.

An appropriate response to God's gift of life and salvation is to commit one's total life to serve God and others. The young boy with the five loaves and two fishes gave all he had to Jesus. Jesus blessed what he gave and multiplied this gift a thousandfold. Being a good steward is recognizing that all of life is a gift from God. Our time, our abilities, our money—all we have we receive from God. In response to such lavish generosity, we are called to use our gifts responsibly and to share them freely with others.

This particular priority is not only about money, but it

definitely includes money. In North American culture, what we do with our money has become a private matter. We hesitate to let others know how much money we have and may become defensive if anyone challenges us about how we are spending it. Being able to discuss this topic openly and challenge ourselves and each other to become more faithful in our use of finances is an important aspect of this priority. (See chapter 16.)

The **Kern Road Mennonite Church,** South Bend, Indiana, has encouraged monetary pledging since its beginning in 1962. However, this practice became more intentional and intensive in recent years. During late fall, one or two Sundays are devoted to teaching about stewardship. Attenders are invited to sign a pledge with three components:

First, they are invited to become regular givers rather than giving only at the end of the year.

Second, they are challenged to give one percent more than they gave the previous year.

Third, they are encouraged to write down the amount they intend to give that year. Children, youth, and adults are all invited to commit to one or more parts of this pledge.

The budget for the coming year is based on these pledges, an external sign of an internal commitment. Most participants believe their pledge helps keep them accountable for something they want to do. According to Pastor David Sutter, congregational giving has more than doubled in the past seven years (attendance has also increased significantly). Giving is more consistent throughout the year, and the congregation usually exceeds its budget. Then they experience the joy of deciding what they will do with the surplus of funds.

Community: Priorities about how we grow as communities of grace, joy, and peace

3. To call and nurture congregational leaders for ministry in a changing environment.

It's not easy to serve as a congregational leader. Expectations of leaders are diverse and often conflicting. Yet the vitality of the church depends on leadership. To meet the leadership needs of the church in the coming decade, many leaders must be called forth from within congregations.

For the past decade, **St. Jacobs (Ontario) Mennonite Church** has used a variety of approaches to call out young leaders from its midst. For several years, five young adults were invited to be participants of a group that met regularly to talk about pastoral ministry. Each person had an assignment in the church for a year. They met with the group and a pastor to discuss their involvement, to explore issues the church was facing, and to learn what ministers do. Some of them went on for further training and have since entered pastoral ministry. Others remained active volunteers and did not choose to pursue pastoral ministry.

In more recent years, the church has decided to test a call to the ministry with one young adult at a time. Each year the pastors in consultation with the pastoral committee invite one young adult with leadership gifts to serve as a pastoral intern for several months (usually during the summer). The intern is expected to give about five to eight hours per week to ministry and become involved in visitation, worship leading, preaching, and committees. Their work is closely supervised and discussed during biweekly meetings with one of the pastors.

4. Practice love, forgiveness, and hospitality that affirms our diversity and heals our brokenness.

A song says, "They will know we are Christians by our

love." Do we live that way? Everyone needs a place of refuge, a place where they feel loved and accepted, where it is safe to talk about the hurts that have been experienced, and where sins are forgiven and wrongs made right.

A story from Comunidad De Fe, an Hispanic Mennonite Church on the south side of Chicago, illustrates this priority. The church, with an average attendance of seventy five, is a diverse group of Mexicans, Colombians, Central Americans, and Anglos. A growth group meets in Miguel's basement every Thursday night to study God's Word; encourage one another; and fellowship over Mexican bread, Colombian tamales, or peanut butter cookies.

Miguel became a Christian in prison in 1990. He started to attend Communidad De Fe after his release in 1992 and began giving leadership to this growing group. With his wife, Esthela, he offered the gift of hospitality and welcomed all who came. During a study of the story of Jacob and Esau and their reconciliation, Miguel remembered Rafael, an informer who caused his imprisonment. While he was in prison, he had looked forward to getting revenge when he was released. Rafael and his family had lived in fear ever since Miguel's release. Instead of revenge, Miguel chose to become reconciled and became instrumental in getting Rafael involved in a drug rehabilitation program and the Bible study group.

Mission: Priorities about how we live as people of healing and hope

5. Invite others to faith in Jesus Christ.

As we become attuned to the way God works in our lives and become more conscious of God's goodness, we are motivated to share God's good news with others. Often simple gestures of friendship and acts of hospitality open the way for sharing our faith.

In October 1992, twenty-nine adults attended the first

worship service at **Wellspring Christian Fellowship** in Clearbrook, British Columbia. By the summer of 1995, more than one hundred adults were meeting for worship on Sunday morning. Gary Loewen, pastor, attributes the growth in numbers to cell groups, which meet weekly and reach out actively to the unchurched. Ideally, these cell groups will multiply every six months and continue to grow. The emphasis in the cell group is on meeting needs and caring for one another, not developing programs or expecting members to attend many meetings.

One member, Christa, had no idea how to reach out when she was asked by her pastor to contact Denise, a first-time attender. With a plate of cookies, she went to visit and ended up staying several hours. They found they had much in common. This visit made all the difference to Denise, who not only continues to worship at Wellspring, but also joined the cell group to which Christa belonged.

6. Seek God's peace in our homes, work, neighborhoods, and the world.

Daily we find ourselves in places where we occasionally or regularly experience conflict, tension, brokenness, and even violence. God's desire is for us to find ways of living at peace with each other, to turn hatred into love, and to move people toward wholeness and harmony.

Can youth who feel marginalized in their community be empowered by a congregational youth ministry effort? Jonathan Brown of the **Church Without Walls** in Elkhart, Indiana, has found a way to allow the voice of youth to be heard in their community through the publication of a quarterly newsletter called *Youth for Community Change*. In the periodical, they share their thoughts and feelings about what is going on in their lives and then distribute these newsletters through the schools. By working together and expressing their dreams, they bring positive changes and hope to their community.

Youth meet regularly at the Worship and Community Center to talk about concerns they have such as drug and alcohol abuse, stress, and other pressures. Educational programs are launched in response to needs. Youth have been learning about desktop publishing, photography, and interviewing. A part of their program includes a college preparation class where youth are brought to the campus of Goshen College and introduced to the opportunities available to them. This congregation has empowered youth to make a difference in their community and to expand their personal horizons and opportunities.

Congregational Checkup

With your leadership team or discussion group, create or review and perhaps revise the vision statement for your congregation. See Appendix 2 for examples of what some congregations have done.

Begin by asking, "What is the vision that God is calling our congregation to embrace?" One way to create a vision statement is to ask the group to consider what they would like people who are not part of their congregation to say about the church. (This exercise could be done in a large group or in several smaller groups).

Step 1.

Ask the group: "If you overheard a group of people in the local coffee shop talking about your congregation, what would you like to hear?" Write the statements on newsprint or a chalkboard. Examples of possible responses:
• They really take care of one another.
• They are people who follow Christ.
• They are always willing to help.

Option 1: If your congregation already has a vision statement:

Step 2a.

Provide a copy of the current vision statement for everyone, or place it on an overhead. Provide a copy of Vision: Healing and Hope for the group. Note the similarities between your congregational vision statement and the denominational statement, Vision: Healing and Hope.

Step 3a.

Using your responses in step 1 and the two vision statements you are working with, ask whether any changes or fine-tuning in the current vision statement are desirable. If you want to make changes, revise the congregation's vision statement.

Option 2: If your congregation does not have a vision statement:

Step 2b.

Take time to write such a statement or discuss the possibility of accepting Vision: Healing and Hope as the vision God is calling you to embrace. Be sure that the ideas from the statements you wrote in step 1 are included in your vision statement.

Step 3b.

Choose a time to share your vision statement in written form with the rest of the congregation and invite response. Incorporate these suggestions and ideas into the final draft.

Priorities and Strategies: Discussion and Discernment

Reflection and Discussion on Priority 1— Spirituality

What spiritual disciplines are shaping the lives of members in your congregation? Of the three disciplines mentioned (prayer, worship, study of the Scriptures), which one is most evident in the lives of members? Which spiritual discipline do you want to nurture intentionally during the next year? Develop a plan for choosing and implementing a priority.

Reflection and Discussion on Priority 2—Stewardship

What does it mean for us to offer all we are and have to God? Do members in your congregation talk openly about their incomes and how they spend their money? How can we help one another to become more accountable in the use of money? What would it take to implement a pledge program as practiced in the Kern Road Mennonite Church? Is tithing realistic? What would happen if everyone in Mennonite churches tithed? In addition to giving money, in what other areas might members be challenged to give more generously?

Reflection and Discussion on Priority 3—Leadership

What is it like to be a leader in your congregation? How are leaders supported and cared for? Are new leaders called out and given opportunities to exercise their gifts? Specifically, are young people being given an opportunity to test a call to pastoral ministry? What more could you do to encourage members to develop their gifts of leadership?

Reflection and Discussion on Priority 4—Community

Is your congregation a safe place to be? How do members care for and support one another? Have any broken relationships been reconciled in your church during the past year? Are participants respected in spite of their differences? Are conflict resolution skills practiced and taught? What can your church do to encourage reconciliation and healing? What rituals or celebrations might be needed?

Reflection and Discussion on Priority 5—Evangelism

How are you sharing your life and faith so others will be attracted to make a commitment to Jesus Christ? Have you invited anyone in your circle of friends or in your work world to attend worship with you? In what specific ways can your congregation become more intentional about inviting and including newcomers in your church community?

Reflection and Discussion on Priority 6—Peace and Reconciliation

Who are the marginalized in your church or neighborhood? Are members actively seeking peace and justice and finding ways to empower others? In what specific ways can we experience greater harmony in our homes? At work? In our neighborhoods? In the world?

Priorities and Strategies: Taking Action

Make a copy of Chart 5, next page, which follows for each participant in your discussion. As you reflect on these priorities, summarize and write in the "Congregational Realities" column what your congregation is now doing to work at each priority. Next try to agree about one or two priorities that need immediate attention in your congregation. Write those in the "Congregational Priorities" column. Discuss how you might work at these priorities during the next year. Write your ideas in the "Congregational Strategies" column.

When your leaders and congregation have concluded the work of writing a vision and selecting priorities, invite someone in the congregation to interpret the vision and goals in a banner or mural. Display the vision where it can be seen often and referred to by committees and leaders.

Develop a version of the vision and priorities that can be easily read in worship services or leadership meetings. Incorporate it into prayers. If you have creative composers, invite them to set the text to music so it can be sung.

Chart 5

Congregational Discipling	Vision: Healing and Hope Priorities	Congregational Realities	Congregational Priorities	Congregational Strategies
Worship: The way we relate to God.	1. Enrich our prayer, worship, and study of the scriptures. 2. Offer all that we are and have to God.			
Community: The way we relate to the people of God.	3. Call and nurture congregational leaders for ministry in a changing environment. 4. Practice love, forgiveness and hospitality that affirms our diversity and heals our brokenness.			
Mission: The way we relate to the world.	5. Invite others to faith in Jesus Christ. 6. Seek God's peace in our homes, work, neighborhoods and the world.			

Vision: Healing and Hope builds on the General Conference Mennonite Church goals and on the Mennonite Church's Vision 95. It envisions the kind of church we want to become as we approach the twenty first century. Through discernment of needs, we are invited to respond by giving attention to six priorities in three arenas of congregational life.

To the extent that we are able to embrace Vision: Healing and Hope and work with the priorities, the congregations of the General Conference Mennonite Church and the Mennonite Church will be empowered to make disciples and to bring healing and hope to a broken world.

For further reading and study:

Transforming Congregations for the Future by Loren B. Mead. Alban Institute, 1994.

Chapter 9

Discipling Children in the Faith Community

by Eleanor Snyder

Everyone in the church—whether child, youth, or adult—is influenced by the discipling ministries of the congregation. This chapter draws its inspiration from the familiar scene of Jesus welcoming the children (Mark 10:13-16). By taking the children in his arms and blessing them, Jesus provided the church with its basic posture and strategy for discipling children.

Characteristics of Children

like to question
are creative
love to learn
believe God is good
like to discover
value relationships
enjoy adults
want to feel safe

innate sense of justice
need love and trust
can know God
have high energy
love stories
are naturally curious
want to belong
accept mystery of God

Ben Gibson

Nurturing Spirituality in Children

Spirituality has to do with an ongoing personal relationship with God. It is a covenantal relationship initiated by God with us. Our responsibility as teachers, parents, mentors, and pastors is to help children receive and respond to God's invitation to covenant: i.e., God's unconditional, personal love for each one as expressed through the prophet Isaiah: "I have called you by name, you are mine . . . Because you are precious in my sight, and honored, and I love you" (Isaiah 43: 1, 4, NRSV).

Spirituality embraces all areas of life. The Shema (Deuteronomy 6:4-9) and the great commandment (Mark 12:28-31) invite us to love God with our whole being—heart, soul, mind, strength and body. The child's spiritual learning environment is everywhere and anytime. The church's goal is to help children "fall in love" with God, the One who first loved them, who calls them by name and values each one.

Spirituality is meant to be a joyful journey that begins with birth and lasts a lifetime. As companions and guides on this journey, the church needs to remember:

First, we must appreciate and accept children for who they are.

Children are full human beings. They are to be treated as neither adults-to-be nor depraved souls. We respect, affirm, and honor their capacity to love and enjoy God. We realize their innocence, vulnerability, and dependence. We learn much about relating with God when we observe and pay attention to our children. We remember that Jesus held up the child as a model for participation in God's realm (Mark 10:13-16).

Second, we must not stand in the way of the child's relationship with God.

It is tempting to force our adult experience and language

upon children. This happens when we insist upon a certain type of "conversion," when we do not validate their expressions of faith, and when we negate or ignore their experiences of God.

Children have a way of knowing God without our intervention. In fact, they may be more attuned to the mystery ✓ of God in their lives than many adults are. We can be attentive to their God-talk and offer opportunities for the child and God to be in relationship with one another. When we wonder together about the Bible stories in Sunday school and when we invite personal responses to the story through prayer, art, visual symbols, music, writing, and story, we affirm the child's ability to communicate directly and adequately with God. When we make time for the child to be alone with God, we honor and invite an intimate friendship with God.

Third, we need to know our children.

Developing a friendship with each child is the best way to invite conversations about God. When we show we care enough to listen without judgment, children will be comfortable in expressing their longings and feelings toward God. Friendships take time, but they are invaluable in nurturing spirituality.

Fourth, we need to know God.

Children are good imitators. "What you do speaks so loudly I can't hear what you say" implies that how we live out our own relationship with God will have a greater impact on children than anything we say about it. In answering the question, "Will our children have faith?" John Westerhoff, a veteran church educator, says, "Yes! If we have faith and are faithful."

Ways to Nurture the Spirit in the Child

"When your children ask you in time to come, 'What is

the meaning of...', then you shall say to your children . . ." (Deuteronomy 6:20-21). In the Hebrew tradition, parents told about God's wonderful activity when their children asked. Family rituals and lifestyle prompted the questions. This text suggests that adults walk with children on the journey of faith at the child's own pace in accordance with the child's unique quest. Our role as parents and educators is to affirm, encourage, support, and befriend them along the way. We can honor and respect the spirituality of the child within the church community in these ways.

1. For Young Children

a. Help the little ones "become conscious of and attentive to the voice that is calling them by name. This voice calls them to be before it calls them to do," writes Sofia Cavalletti in *The Good Shepherd and the Child* (New York: Don Bosco Multimedia, 1994, P. 84).

b. Remind them often of God's love. Be God's loving arms and lap. Enjoy God with them, and wonder and celebrate God's constant love by singing songs they know, encouraging movement, and welcoming them in worship settings.

c. Have regular blessings for young children that remind them of God's love and our acceptance. Give them a real sense of belonging in God's realm.

d. Pray for and with them during Sunday school and in corporate prayers of the congregation. Honor their expressions of faith without laughter or correction.

e. Remember congregational promises, given at the parent-child service of blessing, to share in the child's nurture and well-being. Find practical ways to keep those promises.

2. For Older Children

a. Model forgiveness. As children develop morally, we communicate that God not only loves, nurtures, and protects, but also forgives. If children know God as loving and accepting, even though they make mistakes, their responses to the ongoing invitation of Jesus to follow him will be made out of love, not fear.

b. Tell them about your relationship with God in a simple, open fashion. Be willing to admit your failures and experiences of God's forgiveness. Invite children to do the same.

c. Talk about times when God called you to step aside from the patterns of the larger society to remain faithful—for example, a witness for peace or a refusal to buy something just because others were buying it.

d. Set aside time alone with each child for friendship building. Over ice cream or hot dogs, share thoughts and questions about God. Respect their vulnerability by keeping their confidences. Assure them you will do so.

e. Encourage children to participate actively in worship leading through singing, Scripture reading, drama, praying, and receiving the offering. Make them feel welcome in all church activities and graciously accept their participation. Let their presence and participation change congregational worship.

f. If a child wishes to tell of a special, transforming encounter with Jesus, encourage public recognition with a worship ritual. Actions suggested may be to: light a candle; offer a blessing and prayer; share a poem, song, or litany; or find other ways to celebrate God's ongoing transforming activity.

3. For Adolescents

a. As adolescence arrives, junior youth can relate to God as Personal Guide who helps them make important decisions about life.

b. Discuss theology together. Invite them to explore their relationship with God with both head and heart. Don't be afraid to admit you do not have all of the answers. Help them to live with the questions. Share your faith story with them openly and honestly.

c. Gently and often remind youth that God longs for their friendship and allegiance and waits patiently and lovingly for them even when they miss the mark. Tell them God is willing to forgive them again and again.

As they become more aware of the nudging of the Holy Spirit in their lives, give clear messages about the meaning of baptism and church membership; invite them to continue to say "yes" to God's call to follow Christ in all of life.

d. Celebrate faith transitions publicly with a worship ritual (see suggestions earlier) or a gift of a Bible, devotional book, plaque, poster, or another symbol of their growing friendship with God.

e. Invite each adolescent to choose a mentor who will walk with him or her as a special friend through the teen years as he or she makes significant choices about lifestyle, vocation, and relationships with peers, family, church community and God.

f. Our time, affirmation, unconditional love, and acceptance are the best faith gifts we can give our children as we model the way of Jesus way for them.

Tips for Pastors on Valuing Children

1. *Learn to know each child by name.*
2. *Speak to the children each week, if possible.*
3. *Regularly tell the children's story in age appropriate terms (not as a pre-sermon sermon for adults).*
4. *Participate in children's ministry areas whenever possible (vacation Bible school, club programs, Sunday school).*
5. *Remember to include children's concerns in the pastoral prayer*

Sermon Suggestions

6. *Use sermon illustrations that relate to children.*
7. *Divide your sermon into shorter segments, interspersed with song, litany, or action.*

8. *Use visual symbols as illustrations.*
9. *Speak directly to the children. Do not assume that they are tuned out.*

A Wholistic Approach to Children's Ministry

Everything we do with children is Christian education. Sunday school, club activity, worship time, vacation Bible school, camp programs—all reflect a certain theological perspective and offer potential for discipling. It is important that the church promote a consistent theology in all arenas of children's ministry. In addition, the theology expressed in curriculum choices must be consistent with the theology of the congregation as experienced in its worship, community, and mission.

Anabaptist curriculum for children promotes a wholistic approach to life and faith in age-appropriate ways. Jubilee: God's Good News (Sunday school curriculum), Venture Clubs, (the club program), Living Stones Series and Herald Press summer Bible school curricula (vacation Bible schools), and Fast Lane Bible Studies (junior youth groups) articulate Anabaptist theology. Children are invited to follow Jesus in ways that are suitable for their developmental stage. They are invited to wonder and reflect on God's ways in the world. They are invited to "learn and grow together, to discover the power of the Holy Spirit to form faith, inform minds, and transform lives."

One way to ensure that children's needs are being respected is to implement a children's ministry team. This team oversees all aspects of congregational ministry with children: Sunday school, club program, camp involvement, daycare program, vacation Bible school, mentoring program, children's participation in worship, etc. The team also acts as an advocate for children in the total life of the congregation.

Integrating Children into Church Life

Children remind adults that we have much to learn from them about belonging, acceptance, honesty, vulnerability, and joyful living with a "wonder-ful" God. When adults see the openness and trust of children as well as their delight in God, they see a picture of how everyone in the community is meant to relate to God, regardless of age.

Children belong in the midst of the faith community, surrounded by loving acceptance. Within this circle, faith is nurtured and developed. Parents are given strength and encouragement to live their faith with their children, to tell them about God's wonderful activity, to know what to say "when the children shall ask." Parents are the primary Christian educators of their children. The role of the church is to support, train, affirm, and empower them to teach their children in the ways of Jesus, to love God with their whole being, and to love others and themselves.

An African proverb says, "It takes a whole village to raise a child." The congregation partners with parents to raise dedicated Christian children. This can happen best when people of all ages worship, play, celebrate, and serve together. Learning and growing take place when "we're all in this together!"

—From the mission statement of the Jubilee curriculum (see the full statement on the inside cover of the Jubilee *Guidebook*).

The following suggestions offer ways to help children belong and actively participate in God's realm.

1. Children and Congregational Worship

a. Sing songs that children have learned in Bible school, club, Sunday school.

b. Provide worship bags that contain a hands-on activity that relates to the worship theme.

c. Provide a special bulletin for children with symbols

to describe the actions of worship.

d. Invite them to the communion table as full or partial participants (depending on local custom).

e. Explain what occurs in a baptismal or ordination service.

f. Use visuals that communicate to children: banners, displays, art, sculpture, toys.

g. Use liturgy that includes drama and movement to engage children or invite them to participate: for example use music with hand signs and rhythm instruments to accompany songs.

h. Provide variety in Scripture reading and sermon. These may include drama, reader's theatre, dramatic monologue, or short reflections by several people.

i. If there is a story planned for the children, make it for the children, not an entertainment or moral piece for the adults.

j. Include children in the prayers for the church.

k. Make the children feel welcome with smiles. Give them attention from adults other than their parents. Tolerate a little more noise.

l. Encourage giving by accepting the children's offerings.

A Story about Children and Worship

The Stirling Avenue Mennonite Church in Kitchener, Ontario, regularly involves the children in active ways. During Lent one year, a large wooden cross stood at the front of the worship area. On it were placed hundreds of brown paper circles to represent "bombies" hidden dangerously in Laotian fields. (This activity was a Mennonite Central Committee project to solicit funds to help defuse these bombs.)

During the worship. service, children were given worship bags containing materials for making simple butterflies. Later in the service, a special offering was received. Children walked up and down the aisles offering butterflies in exchange for loose change and small bills. Adults and children both went forward to replace a bombie with a butterfly on the cross. By Easter Sunday, the bombies had all been exchanged—the cross had been transformed!

2. Children and Community

a. Strengthen friendships in Sunday school with group-building activities.

b. Encourage members of the Sunday school class to pray and talk about their faith in personal ways.

c. Plan extracurricular events for children by age groups as well as for all the children together.

d. Plan family socials so parents will learn to know other parents and share parenting experiences and concerns.

e. Partner children from single parent homes with an older couple or single person for friendship.

f. Partner children's classes with adult classes for sharing and learning.

g. Include children in social functions of the church such as potlucks, parties, and camping weekends.

A Story about Children and Community

The Bloomingdale (Ontario) Mennonite Church was experiencing growing pains. Adjustments needed to be made when six new families began to attend their services. Regular attendees wanted to know all about the new people, and newcomers needed to become acquainted with other members of the church family. How could the new families be made to feel welcome? How could everyone become friends? What could leaders do to encourage building community? The answer came in Sunday Evening Specials.

Sunday Evening Specials became a welcome activity for the whole family. On the first Sunday of each month from 4:00 to 7:00 p.m., everyone from infants to seniors met at the church for food, fun, and free time. For the first hour, the group gathered for games, entertainment, and large-group activities. For the second hour, they ate interesting meals together. During the third hour, they played more games, visited, and gathered for devotions.

Each month had a unique focus. Each event was planned by a different group of people. One year each event became a fest: Winterfest with outdoor games, Humorfest, Missionfest, Musicfest, Talentfest, Summerfest, Cornfest, Hobbyfest, and Peacefest. The Sunday Evening Specials drew about 70 percent of the church's attendees. It had particular appeal for young families.

This intergenerational activity built a stronger church community and provided opportunities for members to serve and learn together.

3. Children and Mission

a. Include children in peacemaking and service projects.

b. Invite children to participate in special mission offering projects that involve the whole church. (Make the children's project an all-church project.)

c. Help children find ways to be welcoming and hospitable to the children of newcomer households.

d. Plan neighborhood events for children to which they may invite their friends.

e. Sponsor mission festivals with intergenerational activities.

f. Regularly feature stories of children in cross-cultural experiences.

g. Participate as families in school and community events.

h. Befriend your neighbors through street or block parties.

i. Promote a strong Christian club program as a way to attract community children who might not have a church home.

j. Plan an exciting vacation Bible school as a way to

attract community kids.

k. Encourage children to bring their friends to Sunday school.

A Story about Children and Mission

In "Children here are 'WOWed' into service" Susan Balzer writes in *A Common Place* (Sept. 1996) writes that Work on Wednesdays—or "WOW"—at the MCC material resources center in North Newton, Kansas, is not all work and no play. What, then, is it?

It's a way for boys and girls to tie knots on comforters while they build ties with grandparents, to package health kits and learn about the people who receive them, to break from their summer routines and try new activities, and to get started in the MCC tradition of service, "In the name of Christ."

Workroom supervisor Lorene Kaufman designated four Wednesday forenoons in June and July for the WOW program, building on a tradition started in previous years. Twenty girls, mothers and grandmothers, as well as a group of junior high boys from the week before, filled the workroom on a Wednesday in late June.

"If we do it next year, we will plan for Mondays, Wednesdays, and Fridays all summer," Kaufman said. "That will spread it out more, and I can visit better with the groups."

The WOW volunteers packed layettes and health kits, knotted a comforter, sewed and rolled bandages, cut quilt blocks, and started a new quilt. During a cookie and tea break, they watched an MCC video. They also toured the warehouse and saw donated clothing being baled for shipment overseas.

"It's a great project, a good way to get them started," said Lois Kreider, veteran MCC volunteer, as she worked with her granddaughters who were visiting from Minnesota.

"We came last week. It's a highlight of our week, so we wanted to be sure it was on our agenda again," said Deb Goering, who was there with her two daughters.

"It's interesting how the boys enjoy knotting comforters," Kaufman notes. "Before they had to go home last week, they kept saying: 'Just one more knot!'" "Oh, oh, we can't make any more health kits," six-year-old Greta Kreider Carlson groaned when that project had to stop for the day.

Jumping up and down, Rashell Kaufman coaxed, "One more time!" as her mother prepared to leave.

"They just didn't realize how much fun they were going to have today," Evelyn Harms said.

Lorene Kaufman has also scheduled work days for children and youth to come with their group sponsors. Thirty youth will come from Brownsville, Texas, and Goessel, Kansas, in July. Central Kansas groups are scheduled throughout the year.

Congregational Checkup

In your leadership team or discussion group, reproduce Chart 6, next page, and complete it with assistance from leaders who work with the children in your church: pastor, education/nurture committee, parents, club leaders, Sunday school teachers, mentors, and others.

Consider the positive ways children are already being discipled by worship, community, and mission. Find ways to work intentionally at making children a vital part of your congregation.

Chart 6

Discipling Children in the Congregation

1. How are we discipling children for worship?	
2. How are we discipling children for community?	
3. How are we discipling children for mission?	
4. How is faith being formed in each arena?	
5. How does our children's curriculum promote Anabaptist theology?	
6. How is the pastor involved in the nurture of children?	
7. How are leaders of children nurtured?	
8. How are the children integrated into the total life of the church?	

For further reading and study:
In the Midst of the Congregation: Nurture for Christian Commitment by Maurice Martin and Helen Reusser. Mennonite Publishing House, 1983.

Growing Together: Understanding and Nurturing Your Child's Faith Journey by Anne Neufeld Rupp. Faith & Life Press, 1996.

Chapter 10

Discipling Youth in the Faith Community

by Carlos Romero

A Changing Inner World

In *You Try Being a Teenager,* Earl D. Wilson defines youth as "an adult trying to happen." The youth years are indeed a transitional time when they experience numerous changes all at once: physically, socially, and emotionally. Another writer describes this period as a time when emotional changes cause youth to "feel more but understand less." New questions begin to arise; old and familiar assumptions are questioned; life seems full of many demands and changes. Youth ask, "Where do I fit?" at home, at school, at work, and in the church.

An already complex time is made more complex because rapid changes occur in a short time. Youth change physically as bodies grow rapidly, and not always in a proportional way. Social life with family and friends begins to be transformed as youth exercise new-found independence. They break away from old patterns to create new ones. Friendship and peer pressure play a dominant role in their lives.

Intellectual understanding and the ability to absorb knowledge expand. One day, parents of teens seem to know it all; the next day they seem to know nothing. Teens begin to mistrust adults and may feel alienated by a "generation gap."

Emotional changes puzzle both adolescents and adults. No longer is it as simple as being angry, crying, and—in a matter of seconds—forgetting everything. Many of the changes are difficult to understand, particularly when adults do not recognize important rites of passage. The question "why" becomes common as youth relate to rules and expectations from the adult world.

In their teen years young people often raise issues of faith and ask intense questions as young people recognize more clearly who God is and what it means to commit themselves to a lifelong journey of discipleship. In addition, they ask questions about the church and its practices. Sometimes they struggle with a call to Christian ministry and wonder how to discern what God is saying to them.

A Changing Outer World

Beyond their changing personal worlds, youth also live in a chaotic, unpredictable outer world. Increasing political and social instability creates confusion and fear. Youth deal with complex social and moral issues at earlier stages in their development. For example, society's pressures have increased anorexia and bulimia, common eating disorders among youth. Numerous technological changes from television to computer to fax machines have made the world smaller but more complex. Other disquieting developments are the rising number of teenage suicides, depression, and media support of a never-ending desire for material posessions. Personal possessions are not only viewed as a status symbol but as a symbol of self-worth and identity.

Challenges for Youth Ministry

Tremendous cultural, social, economic, and political changes have made a profound impact on all our lives. Culture has been redefined as the world has experienced in the last two decades such events and movements as perestroika and glasnost in the USSR, the crumbling of the Berlin Wall which led to the reunification of Germany, the signing of a peace treaty in the Middle East, the growing New Age movement, and the collapse of communism. In the book *Coming Revolution in Youth Ministry* (Scripture Press Publishers, 1992), Mark Senter identifies the following trends in youth ministry emerging from current cultural changes:

1. Emergence of non-Anglo leadership
2. International character
3. Urban precedence
4. Group evangelism
5. Student prayer and worship
6. Women in key roles
7. Lay leadership
8. Resistance from the church
9. Parachurch-style church ministries
10. Redefinition of professionalism

Depending on the congregation, these changes may seem very real or quite distant. Almost any congregation, however, will see significant changes in youth ministry within the next five, ten, or fifteen years. In his research, George Barna describes two unique characteristics of today's youth:

1. They believe that tomorrow will be worse than today since adults are destroying the world and leaving nothing behind for them.

2. They believe that everything in life is relative to what makes the individual feel good.

All these changes profoundly influence how we make disciples of our youth. Although the overall goals for discipling young people are the same as those for other age groups in the congregation (to enable for worship, equip for community, and empower for mission), the church needs to understand the unique context in which young people live and the particular challenges of presenting the gospel to them and inviting them to become disciples.

To understand those challenges, congregations need to become knowledgeable of youth culture. Could it be that most of what we see and fear in youth culture is an expression of desperation and a cry for help? Which of the following risks might young people in your congregation be facing?

1. Developmental risk that comes with the turmoil of adolescence and not having a safe place to go and ask questions
2. Family stress that emerges because of the lack of solid relationships or stress that comes with family brokenness
3. Societal pressure to grow up too soon
4. Feelings of uselessness, loneliness, worthlessness, and purposelessness
5. Heroes who are not positive role models
6. Substance abuse (alcohol or illegal drugs) as a place of refuge
7. Negative effects of such dominant cultural values as materialism, violence, sexism, and racism that distort the worldview of young people

It is essential that congregations make youth ministry an integral part of the congregational discipling process. When youth ministry stands alone without intentional connections to congregational life, unfortunate results occur. Youth end up feeling alienated from the church and unable to identify themselves with the body of Christ. The following Diagram E, next page, illustrates this separated vision.

Diagram E

The framework of the Congregational Discipling Vision suggests a new model for understanding youth ministry within the congregation. Instead of being a separate island or parachurch activity, youth ministry becomes an integral part of congregational life.

Settings for Discipling of Youth

In *Blueprint for Congregational Youth Ministry*, (Mennonite Publishing House) Lavon Welty calls on congregations to review the basic assumptions of youth ministry and to envision youth ministry as an integrated dimension of congregational life. Welty identifies seven settings within the congregation where youth ministry takes place:

1. Congregational worship
2. Youth Sunday school
3. Youth group
4. Catechism (instruction and preparation for baptism)
5. Mentoring
6. Peer ministry
7. Family life

In recent years, youth leaders have suggested an eighth setting: mission. Others believe that elements of mission are found in each of the seven settings. The important issue is not the number of settings but that congregations provide a framework for youth ministry that will result in making disciples by involving them in worship, community, and mission.

In *Generation Next; What You Need to Know About Today's Youth* (Gospel Light, 1995), George Barna wrote: "So what do teenagers want as their ideal lifestyle? A church which makes God real, makes religion fun, and provides them with a chance to find truths which are comprehensive and relevant, and which does not strangle them with a list of don'ts."

Implementing the Vision

The Congregational Discipling Vision provides a lens for viewing youth ministry that leads to a balanced, wholistic programs. A first step in implementing the vision is for youth concerns to be adequately represented in congregational structures. Another step is to organize the youth group itself around the three arenas. Three committees (with each youth in the group serving on one of the committees) representing worship, community, and mission might work together to plan regular events. Such a structure might be diagrammed as follows:

Diagram F **Structure for Youth Ministry**

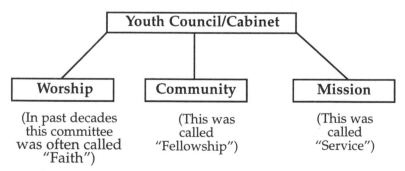

Another area would be to develop a vision statement for congregational youth ministry that is compatible with the overall congregational vision. Some questions the congregation might ask in creating this vision are:

1. How do we work intentionally to help youth meet God through worship? In what ways are we teaching and guiding young people in the development of spiritual disciplines? Such questions apply to the weekly worship assembly as well as other youth gatherings when the purpose is to help youth meet and experience God. What is the congregation learning from youth through their participation in worship?

2. How are we helping youth build a sense of responsibility and accountability to each other within the community? How are we teaching them the community's story and values? Are we equipping them with listening skills and the ability to resolve conflicts? Are we mentoring them in the practices of mutual aid? What is the congregation learning from youth through their participation in community life?

3. How are we helping youth develop a passion for peace, service, and evangelism? What opportunities are we offering them to be engaged in peacemaking, service projects, or sharing the good news of Jesus with their peers and neighbors? Are we modeling and teaching healthy and respectful cross-cultural relationships? Are we calling them to care for the poor? What about care of the environment? What is the congregation learning from youth through their participation in the mission of the congregation?

Congregational Checkup

In your leadership team or discussion group, reproduce Chart 7, next page, and complete it with assistance from those who work with youth in your congregation: pastor, education/nurture committee, parents, club leaders, Sunday school teachers, mentors, sponsors, and others.

Invite youth to respond to these questions as well.

Consider the positive ways youth are already being discipled by worship, community, and mission. Find ways to
work intentionally to make youth a vital part of your
church.

Chart 7

Discipling Youth in the Congregation

1. How are we discipling youth for worship?	
2. How are we discipling youth for community?	
3. How are we discipling youth for mission?	
4. How is faith being formed in each arena?	
5. How does our youth curriculum promote Anabaptist theology?	
6. How is the pastor in-volved in the nurture of youth?	
7. How are leaders of youth nurtured?	
8. How is the youth group integrated into the total life of the church?	

Chapter 11

Discipling Young Adults in the Faith Community

by Ken Hawkley

Young adults, those in their twenties, often find themselves in an intense, tumultuous, and confusing time of life. In their search for meaning and identity, they try to fit what they have learned with what they have experienced in the world. In this mix are questions of faith, vocation, God's call, sexuality, personal worth, ethics, relational and lifestyle issues, and much more. This is the stage of life when career choices are made, life partners might be chosen, vocational direction is determined, church affiliation is formed, faith perspective is hammered out, and worldview is shaped.

Young adults find themselves on a threshold. They feel a keen readiness to participate in life as adults, but some people still treat them as if they are too young. Though willing to try and fail, they may find little space to do so. People and systems want more maturity, more life experience, or less unpredictability than what is assumed for young adults. It's like looking in the want ads and finding that all the available jobs say "Experience Required," but there is no place to get experience! This dilemma leads to frustration, adding confusion to other issues already facing young adults.

One of the important steps toward adulthood is the attempt to make meaning in life. Children and adolescents are given and taught the values of the culture. Young adulthood is the time to begin to assimilate what was taught with what is being experienced. Often this means finding out that some things learned and believed do not fit into the world of experience. The difficulty increases dramatically when the young adult tries to reconcile the difference and has no one to turn to for guidance.

Orienting one's self in society is made more difficult for those who also trying to shape their faith. In our culture, faith often runs contrary to societal expectations and assumptions. Young adults may perceive a call from God to buck the system and become radical disciples of Christ, yet they may see the church supporting the world's expectations. The church looks apathetic at best, hypocritical at worst. Young adults perceive they have nowhere to go with tough faith questions and difficult life issues.

Another part of this struggle comes from attempting to discern gifts and God's will for how to live and act in the world. Sorting out vocation requires space to search, try, fail, abort, and retry. As in other areas of growth, guides are needed. What does it mean to become a Christian construction worker, systems analyst, teacher, or student?

A significant issue for the young adult journey is role and relationships. In the midst of family, roles change and young adults struggle with the tensions of emerging from being a dependent child of their parents. Role expectations may seem stifling when one is trying to forge a new identity. If a young adult's world views and beliefs begin to differ significantly from parental views, tensions may increase until the only recourse seems to be distance or rebellion.

Forming new and lasting relationships is another growth issue. Usually some high school friendships end and new ones begin as young adults find themselves in new surroundings. The need for peer companionship is as high a priority at this stage as at others, but the change from adolescence to adulthood complicates things. Relationships are not based so much on geographical proximity, as in a high school classroom, but are formed more by choice. In dating relationships, questions arise about intimacy and sexuality. When is touch appropriate? Considering the many steps between holding hands and genital intercourse, how far is too far? How can a man and woman become close friends without participating in sex? How can two men relate to each other in close friendships?

Many young adults will choose to marry and eventually become parents. Though they may give a great deal of thought and energy to these decisions, some still feel overwhelmed by the consequences of their choices. For all they gain in marriage, they give up a great deal of independence and flexibility. For all the joy children bring, they also make enormous physical, emotional, and spiritual demands on their parents. Some young adults feel their faith begins to weaken and deteriorate as they face the challenges of parenthood and adult responsibilities.

All of these issues of identity, vocation, and relationships are, of course, tied in with faith questions. But beyond the personal world, young adults face questions: What is the meaning of peace in a world where war is a constant reality? Where is justice when poverty and racial inequality abound? How can the church be effective in changing the world? Why have Christians been so ineffective? What is the nature of God in a world that generally seems to ignore God?

Nurturing Spirituality in Young Adults

A pressing need in the spiritual development of young adults is presence. Young adults need peers as well as older people who will walk alongside as companions or guides for a brief period or longer time. They need people who have confidence in them and inspire their hope in the future. Just being there is a gift the church can provide for young adults.

Presence includes some important ingredients, the first being a listening ear. Churches that allow young adults to share their experience, questions and critiques in a non-judgmental environment are a safe haven for young adults. In a special workshop in Canada called "Finding Our Voices" (designed by Ingrid Cornies and Pam Peters Pries), young adults found a place to share their experiences in the church. Special events such as these could be planned across the church to give young adults a chance to be heard and acknowledged.

After listening is underway, the next step is to begin to understand. Time is required for in-depth listening and understanding—time to make sure that what was heard is the same as what was meant. The church needs to remember that receiving another's experience and faith questions is a way of accepting the person in the community and is a different action than agreeing with them or holding them accountable.

Accountability is another important ingredient. The young adult is not a victim. We all make choices. Young adults may have experienced some negative aspects of church (who hasn't?), but they also need to take responsibility for solutions. After trust is built through understanding, the challenge comes to help make the situation, institution, community or system better.

What does this have to do with young adult spirituality? Quite a lot. Honoring the questions of young adults the ministry of presence—listening, understanding, and calling them to accountability—builds a foundation for growth toward mature discipleship. If the community is faithful at this critical stage of the journey, even young adults who may temporarily keep the church at a distance will be more likely to return in the coming years. Who else but the church could emphasize the need for prayer and regular communion with God? No one can really tell another what a friend we have in Jesus—it must be experienced. That comes with regular prayer, worship, meditation, reading Scripture, and discernment through the Holy Spirit. Growth in such practices is not likely to occur without a connection with a faith community. Thus the church plays a key role in calling young adults to faith and discipling them to maturity.

Discipling Implications for Teachers and Pastors

The ministry of presence with young adults involves not losing touch—a difficult goal to attain with a generation on the move. Two factors make it hard for the church to stay in touch. A *first* factor has been termed "the theology of wild oats." This perspective assumes that all young people need a time to sow their oats and then return to the church. During the sowing phase, the church assumes it does not need to be involved in their lives because it is a period of rebellion, testing the boundaries, and bumping up against authority. The reality is that, while this time of rebellion may be necessary, the church cannot assume that young adults will dutifully return. In fact, if the church does not seek to stay in touch and walk with young adults during their rebellious years, they are far less likely to seek out the church later on.

A critical time for reaching out to young adults occurs with the birth of children. One study shows that half of all adults who leave the church in their youth will return when their first child is born. If the church plans meaningful rituals celebrating the birth of children and offers parenting classes and workshops on the nurture of children's faith, young adult parents will find the church a significant place to be and will find direction for their new role.

A *second* factor related to the ministry of presence is the result of the way a congregation views young adult ministry. If discipling young adults is viewed as a ministry unto itself with separate leaders, sponsors, events, studies, and agenda, then contact with the congregation at large is limited. An impression that young adults are hard to understand and difficult to relate to may effectively isolate this vital ministry. Young adult ministry may function like a parachurch organization—responsible to but outside of many regular church activities.

Keeping young adult ministry well connected to other congregational discipling ministries is essential. The following idea list offers a variety of ways to keep the connection healthy.

Worship and Young Adults

1. Link biblical preaching with current events and relevant young adult issues.

2. Make sure young adults are invited to participate in worship leading through drama, music, visual art, prayer, Scripture reading, and even preaching. Provide mentors as needed.

3. Recognize and celebrate life stage transitions with appropriate rituals in worship.

Community and Young Adults

4. Stay in touch with young adults who move away for college or career by sending e-mail messages, writing letters and cards, mailing the church bulletin and tapes of Sunday services, providing an occasional "care" package, and personal visits.

5. Stay in touch with those who don't move away and welcome newcomers to the area.

6. Find ways to involve young adults in church fellowship. Turn small groups, potlucks, and other church activities into welcoming events.

7. Find out where young adults gather. Show up with a listening ear and be ready to hang around and visit.

8. Assign mentors or spiritual friends to young adults who want someone to walk alongside them in the faith

journey.

9. Tap young adults who have potential for pastoral ministry on the shoulder. Provide support for them to get seminary training.

10. Invite young adults to serve on church committees and be ready to welcome fresh energy and ideas.

11. Provide nurture and training for new parents.

Mission and Young Adults

12. Encourage young adults to volunteer to serve with Mennonite Central Committee, Voluntary Service, Christian Peacemaker Teams, or other service or peacemaking groups.

13. Invite young adults to organize and supervise a recycling program for the congregation.

14. Encourage young adults to share their faith with others. Some will not be ready to speak openly of faith because of their doubts and questions, but others will be ready to do so and will attract their friends into the church's circle.

15. Offer a seminar in money management, emphasizing the importance of generosity and giving to the church and other worthwhile causes.

16. Tune in to young adult concerns for justice. Support their participation in local or regional efforts to work against racism or economic injustice or to care for the earth.

Nurture Opportunities for Young Adults

17. Consider organizing a young adult Sunday school class that meets at the local donut shop.

18. Invite a young adult to serve as an apprentice teacher for a Bible study series.

19. Host a seminar for young adults on faith issues such as vocation, lifestyle, identity, and relationships. Choose an attention-getting title ("Jesus and Intimacy" rather than "A Study of the Gospel of John"). Advertise the seminar in local laundromats or wherever young adults hang out.

20. Start a "Mom's Day Out" program for young mothers, or plan occasions for young dads to gather and discuss their joys and concerns.

Young adults want to hear the church say, "We need you!" The truth is—the church does need them. The church needs their vitality, questions, impatience, vision, and compassion. When the church vigorously supports discipling ministries among young adults, it reaps a harvest of healthy, committed Christians who will lead the church toward a lively and surprising future.

Congregational Checkup

In your leadership team or discussion group, reproduce Chart 8, next page, and complete it with assistance from people who work with young adults in your church: pastor, education/nurture committee, parents, Sunday school teachers, mentors, etc. Invite young adults to respond to the questions as well. Consider the positive ways young adults are already being discipled by worship, community, and mission. Find ways to work intentionally to make young adults a vital part of your church.

Chart 8

Discipling Young Adults in the Congregation

1. How are we discipling young adults for worship?	
2. How are we discipling young adults for community?	
3. How are we discipling young adults for mission?	
4. How is faith being formed in each arena?	
5. How does our curriculum choices for young adults nurture Anabaptist theology?	
6. How is the pastor involved in the nurture of young adults?	
7. How are leaders of young adults nurtured?	
8. How are young adults nurtured for leadership?	
9. How is this age group integrated into the total life of the church?	

Chapter 12

Discipling Middle Adults in the Faith Community

by Ken Hawkley

Spirituality in the Middle Years

A stereotype of middle age is that it is a comfortable, complacent, secure time of life when adults can sit back and relax. But in fact, many middle adults are likely to find themselves torn by the middle. No longer young and certainly not yet elderly, they experience a mixture of hopes and fears.

On the positive side, some middle adults take on the mantle of power in systems, institutions and business. In the church, more middle adults than any other age group teach Sunday school and fill the ranks of committees. Well on their way to maturity in the faith journey, middle adults have found ways to make sense of the world for themselves; they now invest in structures and systems that keep their world going. They are able to hold in creative tension the idealism and vigor of youth and the realism and vigor of older adults. From their wealth of life experience, some middle adults forge a faith that fits what they have seen and who they have become with their understanding of the will of God. Middle adults move naturally to the task of discipling others. Because they are in the middle, some find they can relate with ease to generations on either side. The middle years are also a time when, amidst the pace of rising commitments and decreasing discretionary time, adults take stock of what they are doing and ask questions about its lasting value. They may begin to envision what legacy they will leave when they die. Others on the inward search may—at least initially—turn up a disappointing harvest, or none at all. Such introspection may provoke a crisis of identity or midlife crisis.

While the growing expectations of society may help to give purpose to life, new responsibilities do not necessarily provide meaning. The middle years can be a time when the deeper things of life are edged out because of encroaching expectations from church, work, family, and community. At some point, a sudden realization may shock the middle adult with the awareness that life seems all busyness but is without substance. Lack of meaningful relationships, a marriage crisis, reduced satisfaction at work, and passionless routines may leave a gaping hole. In the midst of such crisis, old faith issues come to the surface again. Many will recognize these symptoms as signs of a spiritual crisis.

Although not all middle adults will face a spiritual crisis, many will feel devastated by feeling they have walked into thin air and discovered there is no bridge. As at all times, the church should be a safe place for their struggles. Middle adults should be confident that they are surrounded by people who will listen and try to understand. Part of the discipling ministry of the church to middle adults is to provide resources to keep their "love life" strong—love of God, self, and neighbor. When the church retains the respect of middle adults, then both discipleship and discipline can happen.

Discipling Implications for Pastors and Teachers

Even though many middle adults remain actively engaged in the church's ministries, others become exhausted or bored and drop out of Sunday school, small groups, and committee work. The church needs to give compassionate attention to them and understand their heart cries. Weekend retreats with plenty of time for rest and fun mixed with inspiration may be a way of rekindling their interest and commitment. Offering individual spiritual guidance is an important investment of pastoral time. For those sturdy and healthy middle adults who continue to live as faithful disciples of Christ, giving creative attention to worship, Sunday school, small group life, and adult Bible studies pays huge dividends. Teachers who care for this group will prepare lessons carefully, giving attention to both the knowledge of Scripture and the experience of God. The middle years are a good time to evaluate and renew one's relationship with God through fresh attention to the practice of spiritual disciplines.

One way to open the group to deeper experience of God is to include a ritual of prayer in every class period. Because symbols are powerful, lighting a large "Christ candle" can be an effective way to signify Christ's presence. Space for silence can be a much appreciated mode of prayer at this stage.

Encouraging adults to read the Bible together in a specified time period (such as a year) can be another stimulus to growth. Some may keep a journal of biblical insights and discoveries along the way. When the pressures of schedules cause people to fall behind, they can be encouraged to modify their goals but continue to maintain a reading schedule. God's Word can bring new life even to those who know the passages well.

Encouraging spiritual friendships and scheduling spiritual retreats are other ways to nurture healthy relationships with God. At least once, it may be beneficial to return to the basics and study catechism and baptismal preparation material. *Welcoming New Christians* by Jane Hoober Peifer and John Stahl-Wert (Faith & Life Press and Mennonite Publishing House, 1995) is an excellent resource to use. A study such as this one helps middle adults return to issues that may have been left on a back burner long ago but now need attention. Perhaps the years since baptism may have been cluttered with so many business, family, and community responsibilities that basic tenets of the faith have been neglected and need renewed emphasis.

Worship and Middle Adults

1. Expectations for worship often change between young and middle adulthood. How will worship enable middle adults to deepen their relationship with God? Help them find new meaning in the rituals and ordinances of the church such as communion? Hear the Word of God in fresh ways?

2. Middle adults may appreciate a mix of the traditional and some new inclusions in worship. The use of traditional hymns as well as choruses, organ as well as guitar, choir, and instrumental music will help to provide a broader experience for middle adults.

3. Offering a time both to reflect and to respond is also an important direction to consider. Middle adults may find that time to digest, think, and discuss issues will help their spiritual growth. Indeed the very meaning of worship may be a significant issue to face.

4. Engaging people in worship is, of course, the best way to keep them involved. Offer middle adults opportunities for participation in worship. Training and affirming gifts of worship leadership, song leading, public prayer, and other activities, will help middle adults contribute to their full potential.

Community and Middle Adults

5. While many middle adults have formed deep attachments in the congregation, others will lack intimacy because of high commitment to careers or heavy family responsibilities. How can friendship and accountability be

encouraged? What changes in congregational structure might encourage busy middle adults to take time for relationships? How are single adults included?

6. Marriages that survive until middle age typically face a new set of challenges as partners age and children begin to leave home. How does the church nurture middle-age marriages? What support do spouses find when their marriage is in trouble?

7. What guidance is available for middle adult parents? How are they helped to pass on the Christian faith to their children?

8. Some middle adults face difficult decisions related to care of their parents. What resources does the church provide?

9. Stability is one important aspect that the church community can offer. Through the community there can be opportunities to foster and nurture relationships. Opportunities for like-minded people, or for people who share common interests, may prove fruitful. Finding ways to nurture friendships and build trust in an important prelude to more intimate sharing of deeper spiritual issues.

10. Social times can also be a time to get away from it all. Though people have busy schedules, they will always make time for what is important. When leaders emphasize and model the need to step out of our schedules and away from to-do lists, adults may be at a point to listen to the call to slow down. Weekend retreats focusing on burning issues, but with an element of relaxation and fun, could have some appeal.

Mission and Middle Adults

11. With the loss of youthful idealism, some middle adults withdraw from life's hard issues. How can the church continue to proclaim the gospel call to compassion, service, simplicity, and peacemaking to them?

12. The maturity of middle adults equips them for con-

flict resolution. How are they being trained to take on this important role in the larger community?

13. Sometimes the middle years are a time of reassessment. Perhaps this will lead to questions about God's call. Middle adults may be open to a call to mission work—either overseas or in the neighborhood. A discerning and listening ear is needed, because such a transition at this stage in life may be filled with anxiety and uncertainty. Though career-path changes are more common with today's middle adults than with preceding generations, such a radical change still may bring fears.

14. Leaders can also emphasize the need for mission work at the workplace. Perhaps a pastoral visit to the job site and subsequent discussion could open up possibilities for outreach in the workplace.

15. For those who do not feel the call or decide to stay at home, challenge them to fund the mission work of others. This is a time of peak earnings. It is also a time of many expenses and more anticipated on the way, such as college and marriage for their children. An active emphasis on budgeting and stewardship can help these adults to become more discerning about the importance of their contributions.

16. Within the church, mentors may be needed for youth and young adults. These may be opportunities to encourage younger members to seek out God's call to mission under the guidance of middle adults as encouragers and enablers. Affirmation from someone older has great influence on young lives.

Congregational Checkup

In your leadership team or discussion group, reproduce Chart 9, next page, and complete it with assistance from those who work with the middle adults in your church: pastor, education/ nurture committee, Sunday school teachers, mentors, etc. Even though middle adults will likely be well represented in these leadership groups, make sure that the concerns of all middle adults are included in the following responses. Consider the positive ways middle adults are already being discipled by worship, community, and mission. Find ways to work intentionally to make middle adults a vital part of your church.

Chart 9

Discipling Middle Adults in the Congregation

1. How are we discipling middle adults for worship?	
2. How are we discipling middle adults for community?	
3. How are we discipling middle adults for mission?	
4. How is faith being formed and transformed in each arena?	
5. How does our middle adult curriculum nurture Anabaptist theology?	
6. How is the pastor involved in the nurture of middle adults?	
7. How are leaders of middle adults nurtured?	
8. How is this age group integrated into the total life of the church?	

Chapter 13

Discipling Older Adults in the Faith Community

by Ken Hawkley

Although it may at first seem odd to describe mature adults as a group in need of discipling, spiritual growth is an ongoing process. We never stop growing in faith. Even as older adults become those who disciple others, their love of God, self, and others continues to deepen.

One of the fastest growing age groups in North America is the sixty-plus group. One evidence is the growing membership of the American Association of Retired Persons (AARP), a group with a powerful lobby that influences government policy in favor of retired people in the United States. Signs of the burgeoning retired population are also evident in books, movies, advertising, and the rapidly growing medical field of gerontology. But stereotypes are persistent for this age group. In recent decades, North Americans seem to have lost respect for the aged. Often old age is pictured as a time of deteriorating bodies, diminishing capacities, accelerating weakness, and increasing docility. As with all stereotypes, a grain of truth can be found in these descriptions, but such generalizations usually prevent us from getting to know real people.

The aging process does result in decreased capacities of varying degrees. Physical strength may diminish, and energy and stamina often decrease. Some people experience changes in thinking patterns, reaction times, and the accessibility of memories. Although physical changes are often most apparent, inner changes are also significant. Ageism, a form of discrimination, is particularly devastating to self-esteem. As one older adult said, "I don't like to tell people I'm 72, because then they start treating me like I'm 72."

As people get older, they experience more death firsthand—of a spouse, close friends, relatives, and even children. These experiences serve as reminders that there are more years behind than ahead. The passing of years also means a wealth of experience may go unnoticed and unused. Because society in general seems focused on denying age (staying fit, preventing wrinkles, and dyeing gray hair, etc.), little space is provided for the elderly to be who they are.

Older people may be more loyal than younger generations to specific brands, institutions, and systems. Charitable giving to nonprofit organizations also tends to be higher among older adults. They swell the ranks of volunteers, picking and choosing to work or serve where they have interest.

The importance of extended family grows for older adults. They long to see and relate to children, grandchildren, and old friends and relatives. Often, though, family members are so dispersed geographically that close connections cannot happen easily. As people age, they may keenly feel their separation from family and friends. Although some are able to make new friendships and find new involvements, others struggle to overcome feelings of separation and loneliness. Memory was mentioned earlier as one ability that changes. While stereotypes emphasize memory loss, the role of memory may be even more significant than at earlier life stages. Older adults are often deeply interested in family origins and histories of institutions, relationships, and programs. This interest and capacity suggests important implications for learning and teaching.

Discipling Implications for Pastors and Teachers

Buck the stereotypes! Older adults enjoy active learning experiences. The popularity of elderhostels, a creative education program for older adults, indicates that they remain curious and open to new experiences and learning. Churches will want to explore ways to alter classroom format from the lecture style. Older adults learn best, as everyone else does, by being actively engaged in an encounter with God's Word and truth. For some this may involve passive listening; for others discussion may be best; others may enjoy more active, physical responses such as role plays, case studies, and applying lesson themes to daily life through homework.

Remember the importance of memory—a precious treasure for the individual and a wonderful gift to small groups and the congregation. Telling individual faith stories can be encouraging and affirming as well as giving a focus on the history of faith. Look for opportunities to connect personal stories with those studied in Scripture. To see how God has been present in the past allows new insights into God's care for the present—through good times and bad.

Explore ways to advertise the journeys of faith. Invite the telling of faith stories in a wider church context. Although some may be reluctant to tell their story, this repertoire of experience has been minimized too long. The church suffers when it does not hear the voices of those with a longer faith history. To hear the joys and sorrows, successes and failures of the journey gives the church a sense of God's trustworthy nature and faithfulness. It provides a profound sense of context, history, and rootedness.

The church must encourage and train older adults to become mentors and spiritual friends with those of less experience. A program arranged for cross-generational study provides space to listen and to tell. We can challenge older adults with the invitation to learn new things about God. Because discipling is an ongoing process, we are always being renewed and changed, always growing into Christlikeness.

Scripture studies can be designed with older adult issues in mind. Who were the older adults in the Bible who experienced change late in life? Who resisted change? What made them act the way they did? Study Proverbs, Job, Psalms, and Ecclesiastes in light of their personal faith experience. Older adult issues include acknowledging loss, loneliness, concern over middle-aged children and grandchildren, and coping with a fast-paced world. The church must be challenged to develop rituals and services to help older adults through significant times of transition.

Because discipling is an ongoing process and covers the entire lifespan from birth to death, those who guide the congregation need to understand each stage and the challenges and opportunities each offers. A healthy congregation equips all ages for participation in worship, community, and mission. The Congregational Discipling Vision helps us remember that faith grows and is expressed by all ages in every arena of congregational life and in every dimension of daily life. We bring our faith nurtured by the church into the world; and we bring our experiences of the world to the church. Discipling is a dynamic process— much like breathing. Ours is the breath of Life.

Worship and Older Adults

1. How does the congregation make use of the storytelling gifts of older adults? Worship can be a significant time of remembering. Stories related to the lives of the saints, of the wanderings of Israel, of exile and return can

be a bridge to significant life memories. The history of God's people may link with stories about the congregation. Allowing older adults to relay those stories is a gift to the younger ones. They receive past memories and become more a part of the community across the years. Retelling the stories brings the older adults to the forefront, affirming their part in the present community of faith.

2. As worship styles change, how does the congregation honor the practices older people love? Their hymns? Their sense of what is appropriate behavior in worship? Their need for continuity and stability? Including traditional hymns and other aspects may help older adults feel at home in a place where they can worship. For those much older, meaningful worship includes the more mundane but no less important matters of being able to hear and see properly. Being conscious of some of the physical limitations of the more elderly may aid in creative ways of including them.

3. Worship can also be a time to acknowledge the losses of friends and of loved ones. This can be a time, too, of remembering and celebrating, as well as of comforting and tears.

4. Mature adult Christians often become prayer warriors. How are they encouraged to offer this gift on behalf of the church?

Community and Older Adults

1. As friends and spouses become ill and die, older adults keenly feel their need for intimacy and friendship. In what ways can the congregation continue to nurture them as they grow in faith through relationships?

2. There are more significant life passages for older adults. These may include retirement, perhaps moving to a smaller home, perhaps becoming grandparents. These may have a bittersweet feel to them. Retirement means loss of status and a familiar work environment, yet it also signals

new opportunities for exploration and development.

3. Community life may become increasingly important as relationships are held more dearly. The church community can celebrate grandchildren, grieve the loss of someone close, and provide stability. Faith questions may still lurk and having a soul friend or two becomes increasingly important.

4. The wisdom and strength of mature Christians is a much needed gift by all ages in the congregation. Link older adults with college age or young adults who are looking for mentors or companions for the faith journey. Sometimes the bonds of friendship are best forged between people on either side of a given generation. Older adults bring the longer view of life and the wisdom of the ages through their personal life and faith experience. Older adults may be able to walk with younger adults, nurturing them rather than trying to shape them.

Mission and Older Adults

1. Many older adults are active in service projects and peacemaking efforts in the community. How does the congregation recognize their contributions to the church's mission in the world? What support or resources might make their ministry even more effective?

2. Care of the earth comes naturally for older adults who rarely succumbed to the wasteful practices of recent decades. How can they be encouraged to pass on their good stewardship practices to younger people?

3. How does the congregation guide older adults to make wills that honor God? What direction is given for decisions related to healthcare and end-of-life ethical issues?

4. From the Bible we learn that God calls us to mission at any age. For an increasing number of retired folks, the world of possibilities opens up as they survey the choices of what they can do. Many ministry opportunities can ben-

efit from the experience, wisdom, and vitality that older adults can bring.

5. For those older adults who have assimilated differing aspects of faith and life into a wholistic way of being, new and different situations may not be as threatening or intimidating as they can be for younger adults. Sometimes their increased capacity for acceptance can build across racial, cultural and economic lines.

6. A congregation that is aware of both the ministry needs and the life experiences of its members, should encourage older adults to ministry the way it encourages younger adults. Remember that mission ministries can happen in our own neighborhoods as well as across the ocean. The older adults are ideally placed for ministry with the aged and homebound. They are also ideally placed to mentor young adults into mission work by walking with them. A shared ministry forges friendships and also passes on the Christian faith in a way that no formal teaching can do.

7. If the call to ministry is not possible, perhaps older adults can contribute financially to the mission work of others. The church should not underestimate this important resource and may wish to search for ways to encourage continued giving.

8. One dominant characteristic in older adults is the desire to see the living faith passed on and lived out in the generations to come. This is a mission wish and a mission opportunity. It is another way of saying that older adults care intensely about making disciples. Their desire can awaken the call in all of us.

Congregational Checkup

In your leadership team or discussion group, reproduce Chart 10, next page, and complete it with assistance from those who work with the older adults in your church: pastor, education/nurture committee, Sunday school teachers, mentors, etc. Consider the positive ways older adults are already being discipled by worship, community, and mission. Find ways to work intentionally at making older adults a vital part of your church.

Chart 10

Discipling Older Adults in the Congregation

1. How are we discipling older adults for worship?	
2. How are we discipling older adults for community?	
3. How are we discipling older adults for mission?	
4. How is faith being formed and transformed in each arena?	
5. How does our older adult curriculum promote Anabaptist theology?	
6. How is the pastor involved in the nurture of older adults?	
7. How are leaders of older adults nurtured?	
8. How are their leadership gifts encouraged?	
9. How is this age group integrated into the total life of the church?	

Chapter 14

Pastors as Disciplers

by Anne Stuckey

*When people look at the diagram depicting the
Congregational Discipling Vision, they sometimes ask,
"Where is the pastor?"*

*The answer is that the pastoral role is right in the cen-
ter of the diagram—smack dab in the middle of the discipling process! The diagram of the Congregational
Discipling Vision is not an organizational chart; instead it
is a picture of the primary arenas of congregational life
and the dynamic process of making disciples which goes on
all the time the church is the church. It is not a picture of
who does things but rather a picture of what is done and
how things happen.*

*This chapter examines the role of pastoral leaders—the
leading disciplers in the congregation, the ones who give
guidance to the church as it fulfills the call of Jesus to
make disciples.*

The Pastoral Role
in the Congregational Discipling Vision

Pastoral leaders have a multifaceted role in the congregation. It is not unusual to see a pastor proclaim the Word
in a Sunday morning service, visit the sick in the hospital
in the afternoon, and help the youth group serve a meal at
a homeless shelter in the evening. It is helpful in thinking
of healthy congregations to identify the facets of the pastoral role that relate to the arenas of worship, community,

and mission and the ongoing ministry of discipling. In each arena, the pastoral leader has a unique role as the congregation calls people to become disciples and nurtures them to mature faith.

The Pastoral Role in Worship: *Priest* Who Draws People Toward God

A chaplain in a retirement home found that her "congregation" was quite diverse in its expectations. Some came to worship because it was the only activity occurring that day. They hoped to be entertained. Many came to see friends. Some only wanted to sing their favorite hymn, "I Come to the Garden Alone." Many could no longer read their large-print Bibles, yet they listened intently. Were someone to ask each one if they believed in God, their answer would be a resounding "Yes." They believed in God but had no spiritual community outside of the one at the retirement home. With failing health and death on the horizon, these folks were sincere in their desire to see God.

In that congregation the chaplain discovered how important it was to pray for individuals in worship. Baptismal services for new believers carried heightened significance. In the retirement home, the chaplain understood the honor and responsibility of acting as a priest in the service of God. As priest, the chaplain helped to draw these dear ones toward God in worship. Even more, the chaplain at times represented the very face of God to them.

Pastors serve as priests of the congregation when they draw others toward God in worship and lead the congregation in rituals which acknowledge God's absolute reign in their lives. Pastors receive authority from Jesus who instructed the disciples to baptize all nations in the name of the Father, Son and Holy Spirit (Matthew 28:19). Paul described himself as a "minister of Christ Jesus to the Gentiles in the priestly service of the gospel of God" (Romans 15:16). So too pastoral ministers are called to be faithful priests in the service of God.

What are the priestly tasks which pastors undertake in the service of God? These priestly functions are most readily evident in the congregation's life of worship. Pastors lead the congregation in the worship of God, prayer, and study of the Scriptures. Jesus performed all three functions in his own ministry. He freed the Samaritan woman to worship God in spirit and in truth (John 4:23-24). Jesus prayed for his disciples that they would be unified and that God's love would be in them (John 17:21,26). He led the study of Scripture as he read from the Isaiah scroll in his own hometown synagogue at Nazareth (Luke 4:16-27).

Jesus also led the disciples in an observance of the Passover ritual in the upper room. There he used the Passover symbols of bread and wine to institute a remembrance of his own broken body and shed blood and to point toward the day when God's loving purposes would be fulfilled on earth and in heaven (Luke 22:14-20). In so doing, Jesus gave authority to ministers to lead ritual celebrations and times of commitment for the community of faith.

As followers of Jesus, pastors continue the priestly functions of serving communion and baptizing new believers. Such an understanding of priestly ministry can be broadened even further to include performing wedding ceremonies, conducting funerals, and blessing parents and children in the community of faith. In healing rituals—whether at the bedside of the ill and dying or leading prayers for healing in the context of worship—a pastor's touch with anointing oil represents Christ's loving touch. In all these rituals, the church acknowledges God's reign in our individual lives and also takes its place collectively as God's people.

The Pastoral Role in the Body of Christ: *Shepherd* Who Cares for the Flock and Draws Them Toward Each Other

A woman was dying of a slow-growing cancer. There were crisis episodes which required that the pastor be there, but there were also long days of worrying about when the cancer would progress to the next stage. Week in and week out, rides were needed to the hospital for chemotherapy treatments. On many days, all the woman wanted was someone who would listen to her thoughts and fears. The pastor visited weekly and ministered to her spiritual needs, but he also arranged for someone of the woman's choosing from the congregation to be the one who would be there for her on a regular basis. The pastor cared for this child of God and at the same time helped draw in others to care as well.

An overwhelming history of theology and practice within Mennonite tradition envisions the pastoral role as shepherd or caretaker of the flock. Mennonites have valued the identity of Jesus as the Good Shepherd who lays down his life for the sheep (John 10:11). Like Jesus, we have great compassion for those who are harassed and helpless, like a sheep without a shepherd (Matthew 9:36). So we have readily embraced the nurturing image of pastors as shepherds. In functional terms, pastors are called to provide and oversee pastoral care and crisis care for those who are in family stress, in grief, in emotional trauma, and in transitional times. Pastors are also required to take seriously their responsibility to engender appropriate discipline within the congregation. In very small congregations, the pastor may be the primary caregiver. When a pastoral team is in place, these leaders also share oversight for pastoral care.

However, the ministry of pastoral care also requires that members of the community care for one another. When a new baby arrives and meals are needed, community care is organized. When a family leaves the congregation or a new one enters and needs extra care for the adjustment period, designated members can also provide important care. In situations such as these, pastoral leaders facilitate caring and provide training for lay people. "Calling and Caring Labs" and the Stephen Ministries have been valuable tools for developing ministry skills for pastoral care. At such times the pastor is also the shepherd who draws the congregation together so they can function as the body of Christ to each other.

In addition to caring for the flock in times of need, pastors also become the shepherd of the flock on a day-to-day basis. In Psalm 23, the Good Shepherd is described as one who daily leads the flock to green pastures and still waters; in the same way pastoral leaders nurture and guide the congregation. By tending the health of relationships and structures, providing resources, and keeping guard against danger, pastors serve as trustworthy representatives of Jesus Christ. When they are faithful, the whole flock thrives and lives together in harmony and peace.

The Pastoral Role in Mission: *Evangelist* Who Draws the Congregation Out to Engage the World

A transient man stopped at the church early one summer morning. Many such people came to that church because of the interstate highway running through the city. The man was looking for the pastor and some money, but he was having difficulty believing that the one who met him was the pastor. So he sat and talked with her for a good hour. Even though she was willing to help, he didn't seem to believe she was capable of providing such help. Eventually he left. After he had gone, the pastor realized she had offered him food, shelter, and expenses—everything but the gospel of Christ. As a pastor, she knew she was called to preach and to care for God's people, but she was also called to be an evangelist. On that occasion she had not spoken the living word. It is true that evangelists do more than simply preach! In fact, limiting evangelism to preaching alone is a disservice to the word. *Evangelion* means to be the bearer of good news in what we do and what we say. This definition implies then that pastors as evangelists draw the congregation outward to engage the world. Pastoral leaders empower the congregation for evangelistic ministry first by modeling a heart of compassion for the surrounding community and the needs of the world. In the prayers that are prayed in worship, in sermons preached, and in active personal involvement, pastors show what it means to love God's world as Jesus did.

As a way of supporting the congregation's growth in love for the world, pastors encourage congregational training in evangelism and peacemaking. The LIFE (Living In Faithful Evangelism) process has become an effective and valuable tool in Mennonite congregations for equipping people for evangelism ministry. Jesus prepared his disciples before he sent them out. He gave them the power they needed to cure diseases and cast out demons. He gave them instructions about how to act and what to say as well (Luke 9:1-5). It is unreasonable for pastors to expect believers to go and evangelize without giving them the tools they need.

The call to "make disciples as we go" in Matthew 28:19 applies to both pastors and lay people. If pastors spend all of their time with people in the church, they are not "going." Therefore pastors need to take time to talk to people in the local coffee shop, join a bowling league or community organization, or play on a local softball team. Evangelism requires that pastors be well acquainted with their community. They need to be alert to meeting newcomers and building relationships with those who do not know Jesus Christ.

Sharing the good news of Jesus Christ also means working for peace and justice in the local community. Although Mennonites have traditionally given strong support to charity and serving the poor, many are becoming more actively involved in local violence intervention and antiracism efforts. Because they function as church representatives in the community, pastors have particularly critical roles to play in efforts to bring peace and justice. When they write letters to the editor, speak at community meetings, join public prayer rituals, cooperate with other racial/ethnic leaders, and become visibly involved in peace efforts, they provide leaderships not only for their own congregations, but also for the community as a whole.

The Pastoral Role of Discipler: *Preacher, Teacher, and Discerning Guide* for the Community

Pastors are readily seen as priests, shepherds, and evangelists in the life of the congregation, but that is not all they do. At the center of congregational life is the dynamic, transforming ministry of discipling. A pastor is also a maker of disciples—one who leads the congregation's ministry of discipling.

As stated earlier, the ministry of discipling takes place whenever the church is being the church. By extension, one could say it also takes place whenever a pastor is being a pastor. One of the most visible discipling ministries of pastors is that of preaching. Week in and week out, pastors proclaim the story and vision of God's love and God's call. Christ-centered preaching forms a foundation for the congregation's growth in prayer and worship, for their relationships with one another, and for their daily life of witness and service in the world.

Another very visible discipling ministry occurs as pastors call people to faith and prepare candidates for baptism and church membership. Even though other leaders may also guide this process, pastors often play a key role in teaching and mentoring new Christians. As they pass on the Christian story, teach spiritual disciplines, guide new believers in understanding the church, and oversee their readiness for baptism, pastors embody the presence of Jesus.

Teaching as discipling also occurs as pastors provide skill training for congregational leaders—elders, deacons, committee chairs and members, greeters, ushers, care-givers, youth leaders, small group leaders, evangelists, and assorted other roles. Each arena of congregational life— worship, community, and mission—calls for particular training. Because pastors are often the only people in the congregation with formal training for these roles, they become instructors and coaches who "equip the saints for the work of ministry" (Ephesians 4:12).

Another key context for congregational discipling is dis-cernment. Perhaps the major focus of pastoral leadership in this arena is discernment of the congregational vision. Even though understanding and articulating the congregational vision is not a pastor's responsibility alone, pastors do carry responsibility for guiding the overall process. As keepers of the vision and catalysts who make the vision a reality, they continually keep these questions alive in the congregation: Who is God calling us to be? How shall we respond to God's call?

The complex and changing North American cultural environment also calls congregations to engage in discern-ment regarding a variety of ethical issues and practices which the church has never faced before. At such a time, pastors need to be able to lead congregations to see and fol-low the Spirit's direction. Such ministry includes prayer, silence, scriptural teaching, group leadership, and the capacity to recognize and interpret God's movements.

Pastors also carry out the ministry of discernment on a one-to-one basis when they serve as spiritual guides for individuals. When persons ask for guidance, for example, in their life of prayer, making vocational decisions, or dealing with spiritual questions, a pastor represents God's listening and enabling presence. Trusting the Spirit to lead, both the pastor and the one being guided open themselves to the light of God's Word and to the ways God is being revealed in the person's life experience. Though this ministry is usually unseen in the congregation, the fruits are evident in healthy spiritual growth.

In a multitude of ways, pastoral leaders serve the congregation as trustworthy guides in the discipling process. They train, instruct, mentor, encourage, equip, and discipline others so the whole body comes "to the unity of the faith . . . to maturity" (Ephesians 4:13).

Congregational Checkup

Before the Congregational Discipling Vision can become a reality in the congregation, it must first be embodied in the leadership team. In your leadership team or discussion group, consider the following questions:

1. Using Chart 11, next page, examine the job description of the pastor or pastors in light of this chapter. Fill in each section with the tasks assigned to the pastor(s). What balance is represented among the roles of priest, shepherd, evangelist, and discipler? Are you satisfied with the balance? Does the job description fit with the congregation's expectations and stated vision?

Chart 11

Tasks of the Pastor

Priest	Shepherd	Evangelist	Discipler
1.	1.	1.	1.
2.	2.	2.	2.
3.	3.	3.	3.
4.	4.	4.	4.
5.	5.	5.	5.
6.	6.	6.	6.
7.	7.	7.	7.
8.	8.	8.	8.

2. Because worship plays such a key role in communicating the congregation's vision and because preaching is an important ingredient in worship, fill in Chart 12 below with worship themes/sermon topics for the past six months. Determine as best you can where the themes should fit among the arenas. For each Sunday, determine whether the focus best fits worship, community, or mission or the discipling process. Then write the worship theme/sermon topic in the appropriate box.

Chart 12

Worship Themes

	Worship	Community	Mission	Discipling Process
Date 1.				
2.				
3.				
4. etc.				

What did you discover? Talk about it. Are you satisfied with the balance of themes represented? What are the disadvantages of focusing too much on one arena to the neglect of the others? Are there times when a heavy emphasis is needed in one arena? Is the congregation's vision being adequately communicated in its preaching and worship?

For further reading and study:
Leading the Congregation: Caring for Yourself While Serving the People by Norman Shawchuck and Roger Heuser. Abingdon Press, 1993.

Chapter 15

Organizational Structures to Express the Congregational Discipling Vision

by Dale W. Stoltzfus

When a congregation has done the creative, Spirit-led work of discerning a vision, and evaluating how well their present ministries and organizations fulfill the vision, they still might not be able to carry it out. Sometimes the organizational patterns of the church get in the way of living the vision.

This chapter looks at church structures and explores what is needed to develop a healthy congregation. How can the Congregational Discipling Vision be expressed in the organization of a congregation?

Changing Structures

Historically congregations have periodically changed the way they are organized to do congregational life and ministry—usually during a time of renewal or as a response to conflict. When a fresh vision emerges, new structures are developed to enable the vision to move forward. Currently in some Mennonite churches, major questions are again being asked about congregational structures. Congregations seek more effective ways to be faithful as nurturing and witnessing communities of faith. The Spirit of God is breathing new life into our church.

A change in structures does not automatically change attitudes and behaviors in the congregation. While not an end in themselves, structures have the capacity to do both good and evil. They can be destructive and serve the purposes of those who create the form or organize the group. Structures can become so rigid that the Spirit of God is not given freedom to lead the community of faith into renewal and a more healthy way of life.

Structures can also be a gift from God to help the body function and to assist in discernment and communication. Structures express and shape values—who we are and what we care about. Structures can create possibilities which otherwise would not exist. All congregations have a need for order and for bonds which enable people to work together. The challenge is to find and develop structures which will serve rather than hinder the vision and identity of the church.

Ever since the boards of the Mennonite Church and General Conference Mennonite Church introduced the Congregational Discipling Vision as a model for healthy congregational life, congregations have asked for organizational designs that would assist them to structure their ministry to live out the vision. While many congregations feel satisfied with their current structures, others struggle with ineffective or overly complex organization. Radical restructuring may not be possible or even advisable for some. For those who want to rethink current structures, this chapter provides some historical background and suggests a process to follow.

How We Got Where We Are

Prior to 1950 the structures of most Mennonite congregations were very simple. Because leadership and ministry tended to be centered in a few people, little organization was needed for congregational life. After 1950 congregations began to move away from clan-centered patterns and developed church councils to assist pastors and to give leadership to congregational ministries. In this business-model approach, better communication and more efficiency often became the goals.

Congregational life indeed became more efficient. However by 1960 many congregations also began to call elders/deacons to assist the pastor in ministry and provide spiritual oversight. While these shared leadership structures have served some congregations well, others suffered because of confusion about the role of elders/deacons. Sometimes competition developed between the church council and elder/deacon group because of lack of clarity about their roles. Care for spiritual vision tended to get lost, and at times pastors were not given permission to lead.

In the meantime, many congregations developed a greater variety of ministries and put in place an expanded and complicated organizational structure to support it. By the mid-1980's, frustration and dissatisfaction in some congregations led the churchwide boards to engage in a research and testing program. Out of this work, the Congregational Discipling Vision emerged.

In response to current issues and looking ahead to the future, the Congregational Discipling Vision moves the focus in congregational life away from proliferating activity to a more focused spiritual vision and ministry. This vision is an attempt to keep the central focus of congregational life clear—making disciples. The model emphasizes the discipling ministries which occur in every arena. It encourages all members to use their gifts for ministry, both within the congregation and beyond. The new vision offers a structure for healthy, life-giving balance among the three arenas of worship, community, and mission. It encourages pastors to lead the congregation to become God's people in mission in the world.

Objectives of the Congregational Discipling Vision Structure

A biblical understanding of ministry is that all members of a congregation are called to ministry. Those who are called out to lead in administrative and coordinating functions enable the whole body to function properly.

Some objectives of the Congregational Discipling Vision structure are:

1. To encourage congregations *to develop a vision and priorities* for their life as a body. This vision would serve as a tool to evaluate current congregational ministry and as a guide to discern directions for the future.

2. To assist the congregation *to clarify ministry roles and functions.* This objective supports the view that congregations should spend less time doing committee work and encourage more members to do the work of ministering.

3. To develop a vision and organization that encourage all members *to discern their gifts for ministry* and provide appropriate support.

4. *To guide congregations toward healthy, well-balanced ministries* in the three arenas of worship, community, and mission. Congregations tend to do some arenas of congregational life well at the expense of other arenas.

5. *To find more effective ways to assist the ministry team (or pastoral leaders) to lead.* The central role of the ministry team is to attend to disciple-making in each arena of congregational life. This model moves from expecting a pastor to have gifts in all areas of ministry to having a ministry team in which a lead pastor enables a variety of gifted people to lead.

6. *To assist congregations to organize their structures in correspondence with the Joint MC-GC Leadership Polity Statement* (*A Mennonite Polity for Ministerial Leadership* Faith & Life Press, 1996). Congregations are expected to welcome oversight and desire pastoral leadership and active elder/dea-

con leadership. The pastor is part of a ministry team and gives leadership to it and the congregation.

A Proposed Structure

This organizational mode, Diagram G, below, is founded on a three-part vision of congregational life which identifies worship, community, and mission as three primary ministry arenas. At the center and circulating among all the arenas is the dynamic process of discipling—calling people to accept Jesus as Savior and Lord and nurturing them toward Christian maturity along with the entire body of believers.

Diagram G

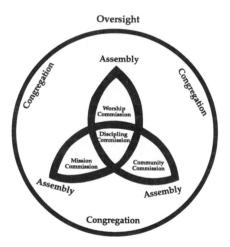

This model provides a flow of communication from the congregation to leadership and from the leadership back to the congregation. The three basic organizational units are (1) the pastoral ministry team, (2) commissions, and (3) the congregation-at-large. This model is adaptable to both large and small congregations and also to a variety of theological expressions among Anabaptists. (While this model may be usable beyond Anabaptist groups, it was not designed with other groups in mind).

Three Organizational Units

Let us look briefly at the three major components of the design:

A. The Ministry Team

The theological assumption of the model is that the pastor(s) leads from within the congregation rather than being outside the system and hired to lead the congregation. The model encourages the pastor to be part of a ministry team which provides spiritual oversight and leadership for the congregation. Each member of the ministry team carries special responsibility for one of the ministry arenas which may be organized as follows:

1. Lead Pastor—Minister of Discipling
   [includes overall vision]
2. Minister of Worship (and Spirituality)
   [vertical focus]
3. Minister of Community (and Family Life)
   [horizontal focus]
4. Minister of Mission (and Peace)
   [outward focus]

In small congregations, ministry arenas might be combined. For example, one person might oversee both worship and community life. Ideally, members of the ministry team would have been trained for their roles or be involved in a training program. Whether team members serve full or part-time or receive a salary would depend upon the size and financial resources and commitments of the congregation. Each minister would also lead a commission focusing on a particular arena.

The ministry team would be led by the lead pastor. Some key responsibilities of the team leader might be:

1. To provide overall spiritual oversight of the team, the commissions, and the congregation
2. To nurture the Congregational Discipling Vision (keeping focus and balance)
3. To give specific leadership to the Discipling Commission and keep their priorities and strategies integrated with other commissions and before the congregation
4. To lead the ministry team in regular (weekly) meetings that include time for prayer, Bible study, reflection on ministry; and to provide opportunity for both personal and corporate accountability
5. To schedule regular meetings of the ministry team with the overseer or conference minister.

B. The Commissions

Commissions would meet as frequently as needed (perhaps monthly). They are cochaired by the pastoral team member of the commission and by a lay administrative leader appointed by the congregation through the assembly. The primary task for the pastoral team member as cochair would be to provide vision focus and keep the work of the commission integrated with the other primary arenas of worship, community and mission as well as with the discipling strategies and programs.

By having cochairs for the commissions, pastoral team members would not become overburdened with administration. The other cochair would be chosen on the basis of gifts of administration. Depending on the size of the congregation, each commission could have four to eight members, serving staggered terms of two to four years in order to assure continuity. Pastoral team members would give attention to the following tasks as they lead a commission:

1. To colead a commission along with a lay administrator appointed by the congregation

2. To lead the commission to discern vision, integrating their work with other arenas and cooperating with the discipling ministries of its particular arena
3. To meet regularly with the lead pastor to care for the spiritual well-being of the entire congregation
4. To become equipped for their particular areas of ministry and supervise commission members in additional training
5. To establish priorities and strategies and to receive feedback.

Working with each ministry team member is a commission of congregational members who are chosen to develop priorities and strategies for their commission and to oversee the discipling ministries related to their arena. The ministry team member is responsible to link the work of a commission with the Discipling Commission. At times the four commissions would meet jointly to project strategies and evaluate their ministries.

Commissions might also establish subcommittees or task forces to assist their area of ministry. Those committees and task forces would function under the leadership of the commission and report their work to that commission.

1. The Discipling Commission

The Discipling Commission serves as the nerve center or coordinating center of congregational life. This commission provides leadership for giving and receiving counsel. It leads in reporting at congregational discernment meetings. This commission provides oversight for all administrative structures. In addition to ministry team members, the commission may include members from other committees that carry out the priorities of this commission. Such sub-committees could include the following: small groups, gift discernment, new member initiation, biblical and theological education (such as Sunday school and Bible school), and age-group ministries. The ministry of trustees and record and property maintenance could be subunits of this commission.

2. The Worship Commission

The Worship Commission provides spiritual oversight for the variety of ministries in the congregation related to worship. Some subcommittees serving with the worship commission might include music, the arts, ushers, and age-group representatives for children and youth/young adults.

3. The Community Commission

The Community Commission oversees fellowship life, mutual aid, and pastoral care. Some subcommittees might include mutual aid, marriage and family life, history of the congregation and Anabaptist-Mennonite heritage, relationships to the broader church, conflict resolution, and pastoral and ministerial leadership care.

4. The Mission Commission

The Mission Commission provides oversight in the area of outreach ministries which include the congregation's witness and service in the community. Some sub-committees might include peacemaking, evangelism, voluntary service, links with Mennonite Central Committee, and programs such as Mennonite Disaster Service.

5. Congregation

The entire congregation would gather at least once each year for the purpose of reviewing their vision, hearing reports from the commissions, reflecting on how the commissions have kept the vision of the congregation focused, and reviewing the priorities, strategies, and goals.

The annual meeting would also be the occasion to

review and approve the budget. This congregational discernment meeting might also make appointments to the commissions as well as participate in other discussions related to leadership.

The congregation should be informed of issues and concerns that will be discussed at the annual meeting so adequate time and direction can be given for prayer, discernment through study, or small group discussions on an issue.

The congregation should be structured so each person who desires to be involved in the ministries of the congregation can find meaningful ways to lead or serve.

A strategy to increase communication and accountability among the pastoral team, the commissions, and the congregation would be to have periodic congregational forums or assemblies directly related to each of the commissions. The purpose of these assemblies would be to provide communication (in-depth counsel and feedback) between the congregation and commission leaders.

Every member might be expected to relate to at least one of the commission assemblies (meetings would be scheduled as needed—perhaps quarterly or semi-annually). Depending on gifts or interest, a member could choose, for example, to attend the forums of the Worship Commission for one year and the forums of the Mission Commission in another year. Over a period of time, members would then become acquainted in depth with each of the major ministry areas of congregational life.

In addition to giving and receiving counsel to a commission, members who relate to a forum or assembly might also become involved in appointments or ministries of the commission. A member who related to the Community Commission Forum might become a mentor of a teen in the congregation. Another member who related to the Worship Commission Forum might participate in training for worship leaders and become a worship leader.

Another way to structure participation in the forums or assemblies would be to invite small groups to choose a forum with which to identify. Although small groups have a variety of purposes for meeting, one purpose could be to relate to a particular forum, learn about that arena of congregational ministry, and provide support and counsel. In this way small groups might be encouraged to keep their personal and social agenda and ministry agenda in balance. For example, members of one small group might relate to the Mission Commission or those of another group to the Community Commission. These relationships could remain constant for a two-year cycle; after one cycle is complete, a small group could choose to relate to another commission.

In summary, the primary role of the annual assembly is to assist the congregation to discuss the vision and priorities of the congregation and give oversight to the commissions and subcommittees. The major purpose of the periodic commission forums or assemblies is threefold:

First, to provide an opportunity for members to have a hands-on relationship with a particular arena of ministry.

Second, to elicit support and counsel on a more particularized basis for each commission.

Third, to offer prayer support throughout the year.

Looking Toward Change

Whenever congregations make structural changes, they are forced to reexamine vision and strategies. Such work is not to be undertaken lightly because it is a matter of both prayerful discernment and careful analysis. Adequate time must be given for study and discussion. Often such processes are more fruitful if the congregation receives guidance from an outside resource such as an area conference leader or consultant.

Several things should be kept in mind if congregations decide to explore the Congregational Discipling Vision structure. Of all the proposed components of the model, perhaps the Discipling Commission is least like the organizational structures in congregations today. Typically, we are familiar with worship committees, fellowship committees, and outreach committees. We are also acquainted with education committees that plan for and oversee Sunday school and other learning settings. But the Discipling Commission is quite unlike an education committee. It has a focus more in common with current elders/deacons or church councils than with an education committee because it plans for and oversees all the congregational processes—formal and informal—that make disciples.

The responsibilities of the Discipling Commission might include such diverse areas as planning for the training of worship leaders, pastoral caregivers, conflict reconcilers, and tutors for an after-school program. This commission might also look after education programs such as Sunday school or Bible study groups (in larger congregations, this area of ministry would likely be led by a subcommittee). This commission is always interested in "how" questions: "How is faith being formed and transformed in a particular arena? How can the congregation be equipped for more fruitful discipleship?" After exploring the "how" questions, this commission oversees the discipling processes needed for faith formation and transformation.

Another important feature of this model is that the size and complexity of organizational structures is related to the size of the congregation. A congregation of fewer than 50 members might choose only four formal leaders—one for each arena and one for the discipling process. Each leader might be a volunteer and would be assisted by other church members as needed. In a large multi-staffed congregation, four people might be hired to fill the four formal leadership roles that make up the ministry team. Commissions and subcommissions would then be chosen to work alongside the ministry team leaders in each arena.

Congregational Checkup

In your leadership team or discussion group, consider the following questions.

1. Place your current congregational vision and organizational structure side-by-side to evaluate their relationships.

    a. How does the structure serve the vision?
    b. How does the structure help the congregation participate in ministry?
    c. Do you find any outmoded structures?
    d. Do you find areas of ministry which are not closely related to the structures? Do any of these have inadequate accountability or support?
    e. How do your structures provide for communication and counsel among the various ministry arenas?
    f. What is your overall sense of the effectiveness of current structures?

2. If your analysis shows that vision and structures are working together harmoniously and productively, you probably will not want to make changes. If, however, you find areas of weakness, conflict, or confusion, you might want to consider new structures. The proposed model described in this chapter can provide a starting place for such discussions.

For further reading and study:

Learning and Growing in Ministry: A Handbook for Congregational Leaders by Ralph Lebold. Mennonite Publishing House, 1986.

Pastor-Growing, People-Growing: A Manual for Leaders Who Provide Oversight for Pastors and Congregations by Albert J. Meyer and David L. Sutter. Mennonite Board of Education, 1995.

Transforming Church Boards into Communities of Spiritual Leaders by Charles M. Olsen. Alban Institute, 1995.

Chapter 16
Money and the Congregational Discipling Vision

by Everett J. Thomas

The use of money (stewardship) is a core discipleship issue. Some church members begin with convictions about how they want to change the world and then give money to causes which will effect such changes. Others give money spontaneously or intuitively and then discover they are personally changed by the power of benevolence.

But what about the role money plays in congregational life? How can congregations shape disciples who understand the management of money as a critical dimension of faithfulness—a response to the great commandment to love God, self, and neighbor?

The Congregational Discipling Vision is helpful in addressing three views of money in the life of a disciple. A congregation is most effective at making disciples when it finds ways to balance these three dimensions.

Money and Worship

One of the holy acts of worship is giving money to God. If the word *worship* is derived from the word *worth* (worthship = worship), then the offering is a way of saying to God, "This is what you are worth to me (or us)." When a disciple comes to understand the offering of money in this way, it will make no more sense to sit out the offering because we gave last Sunday than it does to sit out the singing because we sang along last Sunday!

Some congregations have established a tradition of calling all members to make an annual firstfruits commitment. This decision by each household is a commitment to apportion, in advance, an amount of their annual income which will be given to God. The process of determining firstfruits giving is unhooked from the congregation's budget. In fact, the goal is for each household to think of their firstfruits commitment as a commitment to God rather than a pledge to help meet the annual budget. Only after all of these firstfruits commitments are made does the congregation develop a plan for spending the money (budget).

Money and Community

A powerful dynamic of congregational life is the strength of many people putting their money into a common pot. This accumulation of funds constructs buildings, offers aid to the community, sends missionaries, pays the pastor, and buys Christian education materials. The very process of deciding how to be stewards of this money (a spending plan) builds the communal life of the congregation. Since members come to the budget-making process with different convictions and values, congregational leaders must find ways to forge consensus. If a leader sees such consensus building as an opportunity to build community, then the process leaves members even more committed to the work of the church.

Another important dimension of money in congregational life is the longtime Mennonite practice of mutual aid and sharing. Through the financial strength of the congregation, resources are available for poorer members and for any member suffering financial emergency or disaster. Such sharing of each other's burdens knits the community together even more tightly and leaves members more deeply committed to each other.

Money and Mission

Any group can have a common purse to leverage the power of its members' money: for example, service clubs, special interest groups, insurance companies. However, the church is different. The church must also direct financial resources beyond the membership. The church is called to "make disciples" throughout the world—a third dimension of money. While every member cannot become an international missionary, every member can empower mission by contributing to the support of another person gifted to take the gospel elsewhere.

A second important issue for North American Mennonites is the matter of justice. North Americans are the most affluent people in the world. We must understand that this blessing brings with it a responsibility to be good managers of these resources. It is incumbent upon each congregation and member to carefully and responsibly consider what justice requires of us in giving away our money to those who have much less. For example, a structure such as Mennonite World Conference provides a way to facilitate economic sharing between affluent congregations and poorer congregations in other parts of the world.

Only when congregations find ways to share from their abundance will the church fulfill the call to love our neighbors as ourselves.

Analyzing the Budget

Analyzing the congregation's budget is an exercise which reveals values, habits, and priorities. Using a grid of the three arenas of worship, community, and mission, the congregation can evaluate the balance expressed in congregational stewardship. Because in most congregations this will be a new way of looking at budgets, adequate explanations will need to be given so people can understand this way of analyzing the budget and the purpose for doing so.

Engaging in such an exercise may require considerable

conversation. For example, how does the congregation assign the costs of pastoral salaries and benefits? If these costs are simply divided into three equal parts representing worship, community, and mission, would that be an accurate assessment of how the congregation expects a pastor(s) to spend time?

Might the congregation really expect most of a pastor's time to be given to taking care of the flock and little to outreach beyond the congregation? Of course, some pastoral time will be given to activities which might accurately be described as making disciples (the intersection of worship, community and mission). In those cases, find a total for such integrated time and then divide that total equally among the three arenas. If the congregation chooses, the discipling category could also be included as a separate budget item.

When the analysis is completed, congregational leadership groups can be encouraged to construct a spending plan (budget) for the three ministry arenas of congregational life. Leaders can discern together what will be spent on worship (hymnals, banners, music, training for worship leaders, lighting and sound systems, a share of the cost of staff time, a proportion of the costs of maintaining the building, etc.).

Then they can discern how much will be spent on fellowship and communal life (a proportion of the costs of staff time and the building, mutual aid, educational materials, church school tuition/scholarships, camp scholarships, periodicals and books, retreats, workshops, etc.). Finally, leaders can discern how much of the spending plan will be directed beyond the congregation (missions, contributions to conference and churchwide ministries, local service, peace and evangelism ministries, a proportion of building costs if the church building is used for mission and outreach, etc.).

With such a tool in hand, congregational leaders will

have a very practical experience of working with the Congregational Discipling Vision and will also gain a clearer picture of congregational values and priorities.

Congregational Checkup

In your leadership team or discussion group, consider the following questions.

1. Money and worship: In your congregation, how has giving the offering functioned as a holy act of worship? How might the congregation more fully experience the offering as a creative and meaningful act of worship?

2. Money and community: What stories can you tell of how the congregation has grown in love, in the practice of mutual care and sharing economic resources? How might children and young people be discipled to share their money?

3. Money and mission: How does the congregation express its love for God's world by giving financial support beyond its own circle? What guidelines does the congregation follow in deciding how much to spend on itself in comparison with what is spent for others?

4. Examine the church budget using the grid of the Congregational Discipling Vision. Complete Chart 13, next page.

Chart 13

Church Budget and the Congregational Discipling Vision

	Worship	Community	Mission
Use of church building			
Pastor's time			
Other staff time			
Discipling resources for training (such as Sunday school supplies, small group material, hymnals, etc.)			
Program expenses (including training workshops)			
Support of area conference			
Support of churchwide ministries			
Other			
Totals			

5. What percentage of the total budget is devoted to worship? To community life? To mission? Do these percentages represent the values and commitments of the congregation? If not, how can new decisions be made about budget priorities?

Chapter 17

Church Architecture and the Congregational Discipling Vision

by Everett J. Thomas

At first it may seem strange to apply the Congregational Discipling Vision to church architecture. However, every building is an expression of certain values. Members may find it enlightening to consider how their theology and vision shape the buildings and spaces in which the congregation lives.

We can begin with the distinctives of the Anabaptist-Mennonite faith and heritage and ask: What kind of spaces do we desire in order to experience congregational life that is uniquely Mennonite? Is it possible for form (the shape of the building) to follow function (the activities of the congregation)? If we think of congregational life as having three primary functions (worship, community, and mission), what would a church building look like if the sanctuary were designed and built after the congregation agreed on the kind of worship services to hold? How would the common spaces be laid out if the congregation agreed on the fellowship patterns that would be most conducive to building body life? What would the building look like if it shouted to every passing stranger, "WELCOME! COME IN!"

Architecture and Worship

The first purpose of the worship space is to help the congregation offer their worship to God. The lines of the ceiling, colors of walls and furniture, seating arrangements, and the presence or absence of light all contribute to a worshiper's experience of God and the community of faith.

If we want to experience the transcendent God in our worship, we will likely need vertical lines to draw our eyes heavenward. A high, vaulted ceiling is called a cathedral ceiling for exactly this reason. Over the years, worshipers have found that such vertical lines draw their souls heavenward toward God. For many people, the flow and play of light in a worship space also create a sense of God's presence.

Some congregations wish to create a worship experience that is more horizontal. By creating seating in the round with lower ceilings, members look primarily at each other and sense the peoplehood of their gathering. Such an experience contributes to the congregation's understanding of itself as the gathered body of Christ.

Other theological issues and historical practices also have implications for a building's architecture. For example, Mennonite tradition places the pulpit (rather than the communion table) at the center front of the meeting space to symbolize the centrality of preaching the Word. Four-part a cappella singing requires attention to acoustics so soft surfaces will not absorb the sounds of worship. Singing Scripture songs from overhead transparencies requires planning for wall space that can be seen by every worshiper. Choirs or worship bands require room on the platform or floor space nearby.

Architecture and Community

Some have said that the genius of Mennonite congregations is the ability to draw people into fellowship. Since many members see each other only once a week on Sunday morning, our theology calls for plenty of space for visiting and informal conversations. Many congregations have a fellowship time between worship and Sunday school to provide ten or fifteen minutes of informal mixing. Such patterns require roomy lobbies (for visiting before or after the worship service) and a large area for serving refreshments.

There may be no communal practice more common among Mennonites than the potluck dinner. For some it symbolizes breaking bread together, a modern form of communion. For others, it is a reminder of the more leisurely pace of our rural past. For most it is a time for wonderful food and conversation. Such an activity requires space; if care is given to the arrangements, such potluck meals leave everyone feeling invited to the table.

For a sense of community to flourish, churches need spaces where small groups, committees, or the pastoral leadership team can comfortably gather. Good seating, roomy tables for working, adequate chalkboards or white boards, and accessible bulletin board space encourage groups to work together productively.

Providing adequate spaces for children's activities with durable surfaces and attractive colors signifies the community's commitments to the young. Handicapped-accessible facilities also express care for the disabled.

Architecture and Mission

If we ask how a building can look inviting to a visitor or stranger, then we are considering the mission and outreach dimensions of church architecture. First, have signs been posted to show a visitor where to enter the parking lot? Are parking spaces reserved for visitors? Is it clear where to enter the building? Upon entering the building, can a visitor find signs pointing to the sanctuary? To clearly marked restrooms or the nursery? Have spaces for visitors been provided on the coat racks? Are reserved seats available in the sanctuary so guests and visitors do not need to walk all the way to the front of the sanctuary?

Other architectural issues require more radical questions than these if a congregation chooses to be as inviting as possible to the world outside. For example, many church buildings have large, imposing facades with great doors that announce the purpose of the building. However, such a facade may be intimidating for unchurched people and may keep them from venturing inside. Instead, an entrance that looks more inviting to the visitor may have an over-hang for rainy weather, glass doors to see inside easily, and broad sidewalks and floor spaces outside and inside to accommodate ease of entry. Of course, no amount of friendly architecture will overcome a cold reception by the people inside!

Further, the congregation's commitment to justice and compassion is expressed to the world-at-large by the character of the building. Simple, honest, beautiful materials in keeping with the community in which the church is built signify a desire to be connected with the people nearby. Refraining from constructing elaborate or costly buildings also announces that the congregation wants to share its resources with others, not hoard them for themselves. Recycling old structures rather than building new ones can reflect a congregation's desire to protect the earth's resources and use them wisely. As part of their commitment to economic sharing, some congregations designate a percentage of their building funds for assisting a poorer congregation to build their own church.

A congregation's commitment to mission will also be reflected in architectural decisions to make the building usable during the week and not just on Sunday. Can spaces have multiple uses for community youth groups, AA groups, nursery schools, after-school programs, elder care, Meals-on-Wheels, or a peace center? Have showers been included in restrooms so the building can be used as temporary shelter for the homeless, for Mennonite Disaster

Service volunteers, or overnight youth meetings?

A building speaks loudly about the vision and values of those who construct it. Since many members will participate in a major building or remodeling project only once during their lifetime, congregations need to think very carefully about the long-range implications of their design. Will the building continue to be a beautiful and effective place to make disciples for many decades to come?

Congregational Checkup

In your leadership team or discussion group, consider the following activities and questions:

1. Take an unhurried tour (inside and outside) of your church facility. Then organize three groups (or ask three persons) to analyze the disciple-making potential of your building.

a. Ask one group to look at the building entirely from a worship point of view. b. A second group will ask: Can the building be used to strengthen fellowship and community life. and c. Members of the third group will imagine themselves as first-time visitors to the building and assess how inviting the building is to them. Will economically deprived people in the neighborhood want to come to church?

2. Listen to the findings of each group. Architecture which is most helpful in one arena may not serve another arena as well; discuss what architectural form is needed to best follow congregational functions.

3. If you discover discrepancies between your vision and what the building expresses, can the building be changed so it will more adequately reflect the congregation's beliefs and vision?

For further reading and study:

Church Architecture: Building and Renovating for Christian Worship by James F. White and Susan J. White. Abingdon Press, 1988.

Chapter 18

Peacemaking and the Congregational Discipling Vision

by Susan Mark Landis

"The Spirit of the Lord is upon me," Jesus proclaimed in his inauguration address. "He has anointed me to bring good news to the poor. He has sent me to proclaim release to the captives, to let the oppressed go free, to proclaim the year of the Lord's favor" (Luke 4:18-19). As Christians following in our Lord's footsteps, we also are called by God to "love, not in word or speech, but in truth and action" (1 John 3:18). How does the Congregational Discipling Vision encourage congregations to speak God's peace to both members and neighbors?

The Peacemaking Congregation at Worship

As the congregation gathers on Sunday morning, we bring our hopes and fears, our sorrows and joys to God. Our purpose in worship is to reorient ourselves toward the God of the universe who cares intimately about each of us. This trusting relationship with God gives us the security needed to love those in our congregation and in the world as well as to take a stand against injustice.

The God we gather to worship is our only security. Because we do not depend on governments or trust in weapons of violence, we do not display secular or political symbols of allegiance in our sanctuaries. Our worship services remind us that Jesus is both Lord of all and a model for how we live from day to day. The care Jesus offered to the poor and oppressed is an example to us of how to love our neighbors. The Holy Spirit joins us to our neighbors near and far, reminding us that we are called to pray and care for our enemies.

Worship services include times of both celebration and confession. With joy we come before the God of creation. We also humbly admit our compliance with the evil around us and ask God for courage daily to say no to violence and greed. Inclusive words help us remember that in Christ there is "no longer Jew or Greek, there is no longer slave or free, there is no longer male and female, for all of you are one in Christ Jesus" (Galatians 3:28). Prayers are offered for those both near and far, those we know personally and those we know only through the news media. God's world and concerns are present in our worship. For inspiration and instruction, we need to hear again and again the stories of those who have lived faithful to God.

Worship reminds us of God's vision for our world, of the future when "they shall beat their swords into plowshares," (Isaiah 2:4) and each has "your own fig tree" (2 Kings 18:31 and Isaiah 36:16). Worship also reminds us of God's call to create more peace and justice now.

Many congregations devote a special Sunday to emphasize peacemaking during worship. The first Sunday of July has been designated Peace Sunday by the General Conference Mennonite Church and the Mennonite Church. Resources supporting Peace Sunday in the General Conference Church are prepared by the Commission on Home Ministries, 722 Main St., P.O. Box 347, Newton Kansas 67114. These materials are sent to all congregations via *Leadership*, a mailing sent to all pastors quarterly. Materials for Peace Sunday for the Mennonite Church are available from Mennonite Board of Congregational

Ministries, PO Box 1245, Elkhart, IN 46515. The Peace and Justice Committee of the Mennonite Church (11885 Keener Dr., Orville OH 44667) invites congregations to financially support peace causes by taking an offering for peace; use one/fourth of it in the congregation and send one/fourth to the area conference of which it is a member and one/half to the Peace and Justice Committee. Annually proclaiming our devotion to living and spreading God's peace keeps this focus before congregations. Hyattsville (Maryland) and Prairie Street (Elkhart, Indiana) congregations recently discovered they wanted a whole month of worship services to teach peace!

The Peacemaking Congregation as Community

The community of the congregation is the closest portrait we have of God's shalom in this world. We make "every effort to maintain the unity of the Spirit in the bond of peace" (Ephesians 4:3) as we work to reconcile differences. Adopting the Wichita 95 resolution "Agreeing and Disagreeing in Love" will help congregations learn to deal with inevitable conflict that comes as they seek to be faithful to God's call. The hospitality we share in potluck meals shows our love for each other. In the congregation, God's people bear each other's burdens, rejoice together, play, experience reconciliation and enjoy diversity, secure in the knowledge that God cares for them.

Since violence is the accepted way of the world, peacemakers desperately need to be affirmed in the congregation. Here, children who speak out against war can be known and loved by name, youth who take unpopular stands can be supported, and young adults with skills for peacemaking can be encouraged to choose careers where they will work to make peace. Adults who struggle with difficult issues can find friends who love, counsel, and hold each other accountable. Senior adults can tell the stories of the stands they have taken for peace as they continue to nurture the vision.

The Peacemaking Congregation Witnesses to the World

Congregations seeking to be faithful in living the peace of Christ are committed to witness and prophetic action. The community is aware that this congregation says "No!" to violence and promotes peace as a way of life. The light of the peace of Jesus shines in the community through prayer vigils at the meetinghouse during times of crisis; hosting soup kitchens and back-to-school events when clothes and supplies are distributed; offering conflict resolution workshops at the church and in local schools; housing a community peace center which offers mediation skills; taking part in community meetings to voice justice concerns; and having a peace display at the county fair. The building can be open to community groups offering support for parents, literacy and adult education, after-school programs, dependency programs, and emergency housing.

In Kitchener, Ontario, Lombard, Illinois, and Raleigh, North Carolina, congregations have established community peace centers. Lombard's work in mediation and conflict education is in high demand in the Chicago area as well as across Canada and the United States. Jubilee Peace Center (Raleigh) teaches peace through a nonviolent toy campaign, a peace camp pairing children from the congregation with kids living in a nearby public housing community, and promoting mediation. Every community needs a center teaching God's peace!

The Peacemaking Congregation Creates Disciples of the Prince of Peace

Reconciliation is at the very heart of God (Ephesians 2). God's peacemakers gather to study with the Bible in one hand and the newspaper in the other. The congregation rooted in Bible study and engaged in contemporary issues will be compelled to address injustice in the world. Jesus calls us to move beyond simple awareness raising and education toward acting for peace and justice. Members may find themselves addressing racism, sexism, and poverty. All ages need to be trained in conflict resolution and violence reduction techniques. These skills can then be offered to the community. The congregation that worships the God who created our world is careful in the use of resources in the maintenance of their building and in daily life.

Children and youth need special instruction and support in peacemaking in a world where violence is the most acceptable way to solve problems. Some ways to support peacemaking are:

1. Teach that "God is love" is the basis of the universe.

2. Encourage children to think about how their entertainment and career choices reflect God's love.

3. Provide inspirational role models who are faithful followers of Jesus.

4. Involve them in opportunities to serve—raking leaves for older people, baking cookies for a daycare center, creating colorful banners or wallhangings for a shelter for abused women and children.

Youth need to learn peacemaker lifestyles long before they are required by law to register for the draft at age eighteen (United States). Information for guiding youth in their response to the military is available from area conference offices and Mennonite Central Committee US, P.O. Box 500, Akron, PA 17501 (717 859-3889). Peace and Justice resources may be received from Commission on Home Ministries, 722 Main St., P.O. Box 347, Newton, Kansas 67114 (316 283-5100). The Peace and Justice Committee of the Mennonite Church is able to assist congregations in finding resources in this area. Contact Peace and Justice

Committee, P.O. Box 173, Orrville, OH 44667 (330 683-6844). For the sake of children and youth, we need to keep peace popular in the congregation!

Leaders in the Peacemaking Congregation

Vision for peacemaking needs to be firmly lodged in the hearts of pastors and leaders in the congregation. Unless they model their devotion to God's peace through the use of their staff time and congregational resources, the congregation is unlikely to find time or courage to speak and act prophetically. If the job descriptions of pastors and the goals of key congregational committees do not focus on peacemaking, there is little chance the congregation will have God's justice high on its list of priorities.

Congregational leaders model God's love and peace as they listen to and encourage people. Leaders need to model their openness to change as they recognize God's call to love and peace in the congregation, community and world.

Congregational Checkup

In your leadership team or discussion group, consider the following questions:

1. As a follow-up to the budget analysis exercise in Chapter 16, review your congregation's commitment to peacemaking by analyzing the financial commitments of the congregation. What proportion of the budget is devoted to peacemaking? Have you provided resources for peacemaking both within and outside the congregation?

2. Analyze job descriptions and congregational structures. Who is responsible for the peace agenda? Where is God's prophetic work taking place?

3. Where do children and youth learn about peace in congregational life? They spend their week in a world

where violence is acceptable. How does your congregation make clear that God is love and has nothing to do with violence?

4. Peace groups seldom have enough money for all the activities they wish to support! Does your budget demonstrate an interest in supporting groups working for legislation to help the poor? Those who work to offer legal alternatives to conscription and war taxes here and abroad? Those who work actively for peace and justice? Are your area conference and denominational peace groups well supported?

5. Do your congregational prayers and concerns include global realities? Do you use Mennonite Central Committee, mission board, and Christian Peacemaker Team materials to learn of the concerns of Christians around the globe? Do you invite special speakers or show videos to learn about and keep up-to-date on justice issues?

6. How do you encourage people of all ages in your congregation to do service with neighbors near and far? How is your meetinghouse a resource for peace in your community?

For further reading and study:
Peacemaking: The Journey from Fear to Love by Ronice E. Branding. CBP Press, 1987. "Peacemaking honors God's reign through spiritual wholeness, caring relationships, deeds of justice and the work for world peace." Branding probes the relationship between insecurity, fears, and violence, showing that peacemakers change the conditions that breed defensiveness and conflict.

Pastoring for Peace and Justice by Alfred C. Krass. The Other Side Publications (300 W. Apsley St., Philadelphia, Pa.

19144). Eight two-page articles which develop evangelism that is biblical, contextual, and preaches peace.

Recipe for Peacemaking: Which Ingredient Can You Supply? by Ken Sehested. Baptist Peace Fellowship, Lake Junalaska N.C. Ten pages of ideas about the steps to teaching and then acting for peace in congregations.

Peace Education: Ideas That Work. MCC U.S. Peace and Justice Ministries, PO Box 500, Akron PA 17501-0500. Activity outlines from Mennonite congregations.

Peace Ministry: A Handbook for Local Churches by Daniel L. Buttry. Judson Press, Valley Forge, Pa. 1995. Eighteen chapters with ideas about keeping peace central in congregational life, including preaching, education, arts, small group, travel, stewardship, direct action, and so on.

Acting on Your Faith: Congregations Making a Difference; a Guide to Success in Service and Social Action, by Victor N. Clamon and David E. Gutler with Jessica A. Boyatt. Insights, Boston, 1995. Stories, ideas, and resources for helping your congregation decide what work needs to be done in the community, how to begin, and how to sustain.

Chapter 19

The Cell Church and the Congregational Discipling Vision

by G. Edwin Bontrager

Rediscovering Our History

"The latest thing," "a passing fad," "a Christian craze"—
phrases like these echo the sentiments of some who
attempt to describe the cell church. However, upon closer
examination, they will uncover a way of being church—a
way of discipling—that goes as far back as the time of Jesus
and even before.

Though Jesus attended synagogue worship, he did not
depend on this religious institution as a method of discipling those who followed him. Instead he gathered around
him a group of twelve whom we call the disciples. Not a
band of scholars, they were known simply as disciples,
people trained to build the kingdom in word and deed.
They went beyond talking. They engaged in doing.

In the band of twelve were all the elements of the mod-
ern-day cell or small group: a life of worship, an experience
of community, and vision and action for spreading the mission for which Jesus came. These are the ingredients of
which disciples were made. That is why they were called
"disciples".

In the early church under the leadership of the apostles,

the first Christians were intent on following their Lord and experiencing the power of Christ in their lives. They did not construct large buildings in which to meet, though they might have had reason to do so. A mere ten days after Jesus ascended to heaven, 3,000 more people became disciples. Instead, the followers of Jesus met in homes to worship, to care for each other, and to provide mutual encouragement for carrying out their mission. They also shared in the Lord's Supper. These household fellowships were the basic Christian communities of the New Testament church (Acts 2:42-47; Romans 16:5; 1 Corinthians 16:19; Colossians 4:15).

At times the household groups also celebrated together in larger groups as they gathered daily in the temple courts to hear the apostles teach (Acts 2:42,46). In Ephesus, Paul tried to teach in the synagogue where a larger group could hear. He ended up going to the lecture hall of Tyrannus where he could have "discussions" with a larger number of people (Acts 19:9).

The early church enjoyed both the small group cell and the large group celebration. However, in succeeding years when the church became institutionalized with large church buildings and a hierarchy for leadership, the vitality of the church waned. Though small groups continued in certain locations, the cell as a basic structure with its intense fellowship and mission yielded to institutional strategies that became less powerful to preach Christ's message.

The Reformation brought a revival. Though some of the reformers called for a change in theology, the Anabaptists declared that the very nature and shape of the church should be renewed. Because they were not allowed to function in public places, they began meeting in homes where they worshiped, taught each other, and engaged in mission. The heartbeat of the church was the call to make disciples. In spite of persecution, the church grew and multiplied as people were added one by one, and new groups were formed.

Backpedaling or Recycling?

Today congregations that are beginning to emphasize cell groups are discovering new vitality. Those who are reforming their basic structure to accommodate cell groups find worship, community, and mission taking on new life.

Ralph W. Neighbour Jr., a leading proponent of the cell church movement, does not see the formation of cells as backpedaling or reverting to the first century. Rather he sees the cell movement recycling what the early Christians experienced. He defines the traditional church as having a program-based design because it depends much on programs and planning committees and often a limited number of leaders to perform its work. In the cell-based design, the church's ministry is everyone's task and flows naturally out of small groups which meet on a regular basis.

A recent Gallup poll revealed that a full 70 percent of the population in the United States is disillusioned with the traditional church. The same is true in Canada where less than 25 percent of the people attend church on a regular basis. These respondents believe that most churches are not effective in helping people find meaning in life. At the same time, the church continues to ask if there is a better way to do church than traditional patterns.

An example of a church where small groups became the matrix of ministry is Church of the Saviour in Washington, D.C. Described by Elizabeth O'Connor in *Journey Inward, Journey Outward* (Harper San Francisco, 1975), this church has served its surrounding community and nurtured its internal life through small groups for several decades.

Though the shift from being a program-based church to a cell church is usually a long and arduous process, leaders who are willing to invest substantial amounts of time and are able to be patient while the congregation comes to own such a vision can be highly effective in guiding such change. Perhaps the most opportune environment for establishing a cell church is when a new church is planted;

then the expectations and structures can be built in from the beginning.

Revisioning the church as a basic Christian community offers promise for those who seek to renew the church. The cell church model offers the following:

1. It is the church; therefore it is able to fulfill every ministry of the church.

2. It is a living organism, not merely an appendage in the organization.

3. It is designed to operate on the cutting edge of the world.

4. It is a reproducible unit that can transfer and multiply itself.

5. Cell leaders are responsible for the spiritual life of cell members.

6. The basic Christian community operates every day of the week—that is, the lives of small group members become so intertwined that frequent contact becomes natural.

7. Each arena of the Congregational Discipling Vision— worship, community, and mission—is intricately woven into the fabric of the life of the cell.

Discipling Through Cells or Small Groups

The shape of small group meetings makes discipling a natural outcome of group life. Meetings often take the following form:

Community

An icebreaker opens the meeting and bonds people with each other. Even though the cell group may have been meeting regularly for months, members can always learn something new about each other. Groups consist of eight to twelve members.

Worship

A time of worship bonds people with God. A Scripture of praise is read that acknowledges the majesty and glory of God. Young and old sing together in praise to God. Instrumentalists may accompany the music, sharing their gifts. Prayer is offered, including thanksgiving and inviting the Holy Spirit to lead the group as people are drawn closer to God. Members are discipled and nurtured as they share their gifts of reading or music or leading worship. Such leadership opportunities may not be afforded to these same people in congregational worship when often only the most gifted are chosen to lead.

Discipling

The small group or cell moves into a time of edification. This is a twenty to thirty minute block of time for building up one another and learning from the Bible. Although curricular resources may be used as a basis for teaching, the mode is not so much a mental exercise or academic learning (though discovering new facts about the Bible and God's will takes place). Instead, learning happens for the purpose of clarifying and transforming life values and commitments.

During this time people offer mutual support. Prompted by God's Word, the discussion might center on those brothers and sisters who have recently gone through a loss, hurt, or grief. Another member in the group may be facing difficult ethical decisions at work. A couple may be experiencing stress in their marriage or in parenting a child. Opportunity is given for all to share, followed by encouragement and expressions of support. Prayer in this setting becomes more than perfunctory; it builds on a bedrock of love shared by the group and becomes a channel for the Holy Spirit's power.

Mission

Each cell meeting has a thrust of mission—a vision for bringing God to the people. Unlike traditional church life, the cell church allows for total mobilization of all members. Most cell groups continually visualize the "empty chair," a place that is open to be filled by a friend or relative in need and who could become part of the group. While some churches foster small groups that continue for years with the same people, cell churches encourage groups to multiply every six to nine months. Every group has an apprentice leader so when it grows and multiplies, a new group is born with a leader already in place.

Another way the mission of the church is accomplished is when small groups or cells engage in acts of service or peacemaking in their neighborhoods. When someone in the group knows of a person in need of help (a roof may be leaking or transportation to medical appointments may be required), the whole group mobilizes to take care of the need. In communities where neighborhood violence makes streets unsafe, the group can call neighborhood meetings and help people band together to make peace.

Evangelism happens most effectively in a community of believers. When unbelievers first visit a group, the expressions of love and caring demonstrated before their eyes act like a magnet. They are drawn back. They observe more than they would see through abstract theological discussions; they see Christians overflowing with compassion, being vulnerable, sometimes confessing a shortcoming, at other times forgiving another. "By this everyone will know that you are my disciples, if you have love for one another" (John 13:35).

Congregational growth is a natural outcome of caring deeply for people within and without. The church gains access to people's lives by watching for and responding to their needs. Though some Christians may invite people to church only to fill pews and gain attendance or to allay guilt, bringing people to a small cell group is a genuine act of mission. Their coming requires a space in the circle and time for sharing a new friendship. A relationship with a new person may mean less time for old friends, a commitment to be a mentor, or willingness to help even at inopportune times.

> *Discipleship is woven into the warp and woof of cell groups. Week after week as people gather together, they grow in love of God, self, and neighbor. Almost all cell group churches are marked by intense prayer, mobilizing of laity for ministry, and utilization of both men's and women's leadership gifts. They carry a passion for evangelism with a focus on reaching and enfolding unbelievers within a loving and caring Christian community. This model of being the church offers another way to fulfill the Congregational Discipling Vision.*

Congregational Checkup

In your leadership team or discussion group, consider the following questions:

1. How have small groups in your congregation integrated the arenas of worship, community, and mission? How are small groups involved in discipling ministries?

2. In what ways might cell group structures serve your congregation's vision? What challenges would such structures create?

For further reading and study:

Called to Equip by Palmer Becker. Herald Press, 1993.

Called to Care by Palmer Becker. Herald Press, 1993.

Where Do We Go From Here? by Ralph W. Neighbour Jr. Touch Publications, Inc., 1990.

Appendix 1

Origins of the Congregational Discipling Vision Among Mennonites

by Levi Miller

The last half century

One clear trend of the latter half of the twentieth century has been the decline of Protestant denominations which had steadily grown for several centuries. What has caused this decline and lack of commitment in the Christian church? Though many reasons have been given, a consensus has emerged that the church has lost the urgency of the call to make disciples.

Mennonite churches have not been immune to the effects of secularism, family and community fragmentation, and loss of commitment to Christ and the church. In the midst of such changes, a midcentury statement on the Anabaptist Vision by Harold S. Bender inspired the church with its convictions about discipleship, community, and peace and nonresistance. The church in the sixties and seventies placed considerable emphasis on congregational goal-setting and meeting needs. Yet these efforts have not been as successful as the church had hoped. What is the new word for the end of the twentieth century and the beginning of the twentieth-first century?

It is not activities. Activity abounds: Sunday schools, worship services, food banks, counseling programs, club programs, youth programs, mediation services, baptisms, picnics, Bible studies, and service projects. The question is whether all these activities foster faith and actually inspire growth to Christian maturity.

Consultations on the Renewal of Congregational Life

For the Mennonite Church and the General Conference Mennonite Church, a renewed vision of congregational life emerged in the eighties which came to be called the Congregational Discipling Vision. This new vision began in the regular envisioning and assessment of Christian education leaders. They were especially concerned that the primary form of education, the Sunday school, was too far removed from other arenas of congregational life such as worship and mission. Five believers church denominations held a major consultation on congregational education in 1982 at Associated Mennonite Biblical Seminaries in Elkhart, Indiana. The meeting ended with a call for "a new model of Christian education consonant with the biblical and believers church model of intergenerational transmittal of faith learnings and values."

A follow-up seminar, convened in 1983, focused on one of the ten basic understandings coming from the 1982 meeting:

> There is a need to develop a common vision
> and to create flexible structures which will unify
> the proclamation (preaching, presence),
> admonition (teaching, discerning issues, discipline),
> worship (singing, prayer, praise),
> fellowship (sharing, mutual aid),
> and mission functions of our congregations.

It was clear to the group that a more integrated approach to congregational education was needed.

In 1984 an Anabaptist Curriculum Consultation was held in LaGrange Park, Illinois. At that gathering the first elements of a common integrated vision began to appear. With the intent to see congregational education in the context of the covenant community, a triform of overlapping circles appeared with the labels of mission, worship, and discipline. In the center was "education for transformation and empowerment."

Following the 1984 consultation, a Task Force on Future Models of Education, appointed by the two denominations, met between 1984 and 1988 to further clarify the vision and to test it in congregations. Members of the group included:

> Lydia Harder, Edmonton, Alberta
> Dorothy Harnish, Landisville, Pennsylvania
> Paula Diller Lehman, Newton, Kansas
> Gary Martin, Elkhart, Indiana
> Mark Miller, Middlebury, Indiana
> Lois Preheim, Aurora, Nebraska
> John Rogers, Pittsburgh, Pennsylvania
> Faith Wenger, Fresno, California
> Marianne Zuercher, Philadelphia, Pennsylvania

The Task Force was led by a steering committee consisting of:

> Marlene Kropf, Mennonite Board of Congregational Ministries, Elkhart, Indiana
> A. Don Augsburger, Eastern Mennonite Seminary, Harrisonburg, Virginia
> J. Laurence Martin, Mennonite Publishing House, Scottdale, Pennsylvania
> Daniel Schipani, Associated Mennonite Biblical Seminaries, Elkhart, Indiana
> John W. Sprunger, Commission on Education, Newton, Kansas

In 1987, Norma Johnson, Commission on Education, Newton, Kansas; and Jacob Elias, Associated Mennonite Biblical Seminaries, Elkhart, Indiana, joined the group. Representatives of the Church of the Brethren (Elgin, Illinois) participated occasionally in the work of the Task Force.

During the meetings of the Task Force, new vocabulary emerged for naming the primary arenas of congregational life, giving rise to the diagram which became the logo of the Congregational Discipling Vision.

Diagram H

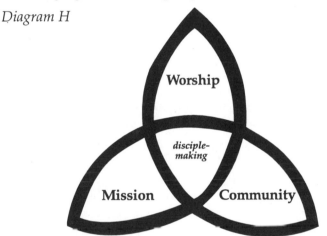

Even though the primary impulse for the vision came from education leaders, eventually the group chose to use the New Testament term "discipling" rather than "education" to describe the complex reality of Christian formation, transformation, and empowerment as the central dynamic of congregational life occurring within the interrelated and overlapping arenas of worship, community, and mission. The group chose to define the church as "a worshiping community of disciples in mission."

Congregational testing of new model

During 1988 and 1989, ten congregations tested this vision and reported strong affirmation for its general features and directions. They were:

Tabor Mennonite Church, Goessel, Kansas
Family Mennonite Church, Los Angeles, California
Foothills Mennonite Church, Calgary, Alberta
Plains Mennonite Church, Hatfield, Pennsylvania
Filer Mennonite Church, Filer, Idaho
Mennonite Church of Normal, Normal, Illinois
Danforth Morningside Mennonite Church,
    Toronto, Ontario
Freeport Mennonite Church, Freeport, Illinois
Lindale Mennonite Church, Harrisonburg, Virginia
Hope Mennonite Church, Wichita, Kansas

These congregations focused on experiments in worship and community, attempts to integrate worship and education, a higher profile of the visual arts, and intergenerational activities. Exhilarated over the possibilities of the vision, they also reported some fatigue from the intense effort invested in the attempt to integrate discipling ministries in every arena of congregational life. They asked for further help (such as this book attempts to provide) from denominational education leaders.

At the joint assembly of the Mennonite Church and General Conference Mennonite Church at Normal, Illinois, in 1989, the Congregational Discipling Vision was first introduced to the church-at-large. Later it was disseminated across the church in what might be called "the congregation according to GORP," a recipe for a snack mixture of raisins, M&M's, and peanuts which illustrates the three primary interrelated arenas of congregational life (see Chapter 1).

Nurturing the vision

In the Mennonite Church, the Mennonite Board of Congregational Ministries carried the main responsibility to nurture this vision of congregational life. It reorganized staff assignments to coincide with the vision. The Commission on Education of the General Conference Mennonite Church carried the vision through a caravan tour in which staff members made contact with each congregation in the denomination.

All church boards and agencies, however, carried the vision as part of their understanding of congregational life. Church publishers used the vision to undergird their publication programs and curriculum. The Congregational Education Planning Council integrated the vision into its projections of programs and publications. Many conference education and nurture committees used the Congregational Discipling Vision as a guide in their work. In 1994, the Mennonite Board of Congregational Ministries called a major consultation to review the vision and assess its validity for the church.

While the vision was new and provided renewed focus, it was based on solid foundations: biblical story, trinitarian theology, and Mennonite experience. If an earlier generation found renewal in a rediscovery of the historical Jesus of Nazareth, this effort found renewal in the pluralism and unity of God, Christ, and the Holy Spirit.

Link with Vision: Healing and Hope

Perhaps the culmination of the Congregational Discipling Vision occurred when a new denominational vision, called Vision: Healing and Hope, was introduced and adopted by the General Conference Mennonite Church and the Mennonite Church at Wichita 95. Though not explicitly stated, the new vision implicitly embraced the threefold understanding of congregational life and the central task of the church to "make disciples":

God calls us
　to be followers of Jesus Christ
and, by the power of the Holy Spirit,
　to grow as communities
　of grace, joy, and peace,
so that God's healing and hope
　flow through us to the world.

For further reading and study:

Perspectives on the Nurturing of Faith edited by Leland Harder. Institute of Mennonite Studies Occasional Papers, 1983.

Appendix 2

Congregational
Vision Statements

Based on the
Congregational Discipling Vision

by Marlene Kropf

As the Congregational Discipling Vision has been taught, discussed, and refined during the past decade, a variety of congregations have used the Vision as a foundation for their own congregational vision, master plans, or publicity brochures about the church. The following are examples:

Community Mennonite Church, Harrisonburg, Virginia
Vision Statement

After a thorough planning process, Community Mennonite Church developed a master plan. Its statement begins as follows:

"As people of the great commandments (Matthew 22:37 40), we are called to love God fully and to love our neighbors as ourselves. We show love for God in our *worship*, love for neighbor in our *mission* and service, and love for ourselves in nurturing our Christian *community*."

The document goes on to elaborate specific priorities and goals for each of the three arenas: love for God, love for others, love for ourselves.

In addition, a plan was developed to strengthen the life of modules (small groups) so attention is given to worship, community, and mission in each group. Thus the discipling process is carried out on both the macro and micro-levels of congregational life.

Lockport Mennonite Church, Stryker, Ohio

Lockport Mennonite Church developed a new visitor brochure to introduce their congregation to newcomers via the Congregational Discipling Vision. Inside the brochure is their vision statement, "Following Christ in Worship, Community, Mission." Each arena of the vision statement is amplified with descriptions of congregational activities occurring in that arena. A section on doctrine also describes the core beliefs of this congregation.

Peace Community Church, Clovis, California

Vision Statement

We are a diverse group of people who seek to be disciples of Jesus Christ. Jesus is our foundation, and we look to the Bible and the Holy Spirit for guidance as we follow Jesus in our daily lives. As we follow Christ together we become one people, the body of Christ.

We are a people of WORSHIP who celebrate God's love, forgiveness, and healing as we praise God and pray together.

We are a people of COMMUNITY who care for and nurture each other as we grow to be more like Christ.

We are a people of MISSION who share God's love and peace as we invite others to faith in Christ and actively seek to be God's agents of reconciliation and hope in our families, communities, and the world.

Pine Grove Mennonite Church, Stryker, Ohio

Vision Statement

WE BELIEVE GOD HAS CALLED US AS THE PINE GROVE MENNONITE CHURCH TO:

- GATHER regularly as a congregation to worship Jesus Christ as Lord and Savior.
- GROW spiritually and numerically while intentionally nurturing one another as a community of faith into His likeness.
- GO faithfully into the Stryker area, our nation, and all the world with the mission of serving those in need and making disciples of Christ.

Springdale Mennonite Church, Springdale, Virginia

In 1995, after being without a pastor for about two years, the Springdale Mennonite Church called a husband-and-wife team as pastoral leaders. In addition to their need for leadership, the congregation also felt that it was time that its organizational structure be revamped.

In consultation with Dale Stoltzfus, minister of congregational leadership for the Mennonite Board of Congregational Ministries, a new structure was developed. It included five commissions rather than a church council in line with the pattern of the Congregational Discipling Vision. Its pastoral team model allowed each pastor to focus on his or her areas of strength in leading the church in its ministry.

Stoltzfus says that the restructuring at Springdale is an example of "an older congregation that was open to be stretched."

Southside Fellowship, Elkhart, Indiana

Vision Statement

Southside Fellowship is a Christian church which

- invites persons to worship God,
- experience and grow in Christ's love and community,
- and share God's peace, hope, and joy.

University Mennonite Church, State College, Pennsylvania

Vision Statement

God calls us to be followers of Jesus Christ and, by the power of the Holy Spirit, to grow as a community of grace, joy, and peace, so that God's healing, hope, and love flow through us to the world.

Vision Priorities

Worship: To follow Jesus Christ more faithfully we are called to:
- enrich our private and public worship through prayer and study of Scriptures.
- plan our public worship so that both host and visitor are drawn into the presence of God.
- offer all that we are and have to God.

Community: To grow as a community of grace, joy, and peace we want to:
- teach our children, youth, and adults the way of Christ from the Anabaptist perspective.
- provide the means for fellowship, mutual aid, mutual counsel, and sharing of joys and concerns.
- practice love, forgiveness, and hospitality that transcends our differences and heals our brokenness.
- call and nurture congregational leaders for ministry.

Mission: To live as people of healing, hope, and love we are committed to:
- invite unbelievers to faith in Jesus Christ.
- encourage public witness to faith in Christ through believer's baptism.

- seek Christ's love and practice nonviolence in our homes, work, neighborhoods, and the world.
- serve the needy in the name of Christ both locally and around the world.
- provide a ministry for students at Penn State University.
- join in partnership for mission with a congregation from another country.

Leadership for Vision
Recommendations: (Presented, August 1996. Adopted, October 1996)

1. That we accept the Vision Statement as our congregational priority for the next several years.

2. That we institute a Congregational Leadership Team composed of current elders, congregational chair and assistant, and the pastors. This team will meet every other month to project vision, focus vision priorities, provide spiritual oversight, and direct decision making. The elders could meet on alternate months for pastoral care or other agenda related to the vision.

This leadership model is to be reviewed at the May 1997 congregational meeting.

Congregational Leadership Team

Chart 12

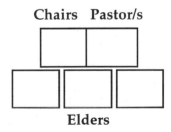

About the Authors

Abe Bergen serves as the Director of Youth Ministry for the General Conference Mennonite Church. Abe has shared the Congregational Discipling Vision with Mennonite congregations throughout North American in educational workshops. Bergen was also on the committee that developed the GC/MC vision statement, Vision: Healing and Hope. Abe is a member of Bethel Mennonite Church in Winnipeg, Manitoba where he chairs the Missions and Service Committee. Abe is married to Elaine and they are parents of two adult children, Jeremy and Rachel.

G. Edwin Bontrager serves as staff of the Mennonite Board of Congregational Ministries in the area of evangelism and church growth. Ed also pastors the Huntington Mennonite Church, Newport News, Va. Bontrager's other writings include *Following in the Footsteps of Paul* and *It Can Happen Today!* Ed is married to Edie and they are parents of two adult children.

Ken Hawkley works as Director of Adult and Young Adult Education with the Commission on Education. Ken participated in the development of the vision into a training model for congregational teachers and other church leaders. Hawkley is currently a member of Neil Avenue Mennonite Church in Columbus, Ohio. He attends with his wife, Louise and their two children, Krysta and Jared.

Marlene Kropf, Minister of Worship and Spirituality with the Mennonite Board of Congregational Ministries, cochaired the Task Force on Future Models of Education which developed the Congregational Discipling Vision. She is a member of Belmont Mennonite Church, Elkhart,

Ind. Marlene and her husband Stanley are the parents of two young adult children.

Susan Mark Landis serves Mennonite Board of Congregational Ministries as the partner-at-large for peace education and the Mennonite Church General Board as minister of peace and justice. She and her husband Dennis are parents of Laura (12) and Joel (9). The family lives in Orrville, Ohio and is active in the life of the Oak Grove Mennonite Church.

Levi Miller is vice-president of congregational publishing at Herald Press. He and his wife Gloria live in Scottdale, Pa. and are parents of three young adult children. Miller is a member of the Kingview Mennonite Church.

Carlos Romero serves with the Mennonite Board of Congregational Ministries as minister of youth for the Mennonite Church. Romero also has served as an administrator of a Mennonite school in Puerto Rico for five years. Carlos is a member of the Clinton Frame Mennonite Church, Goshen, Ind where he attends with his wife Celina and daughter, Elise.

Daniel Schipani is professor of Christian Education and Personality at Associated Mennonite Biblical Seminary. Schipani, as member of the Task Force on Future Models of Education, has shared the discipling vision in many countries in Latin America and Europe. Schipani is married to Margaret and they are parents of two adult children. He is a member of Belmont Mennonite Church, Elkhart, Ind.

Eleanor Snyder serves as Director of Children's Education for the General Conference Mennonite Church from her office in Kitchener, Ontario. She is a member of

the Bloomingdale Mennonite Church, Bloomingdale,
Ontario, Canada. Her family includes husband Stuart and
two young adult children, Jeffrey and Sheila.

Dale W. Stoltzfus currently serves part-time as
Conference Minister in Allegheny Mennonite Conference
of the Mennonite Church. He teams with Anne Stuckey in
the Leadership office of the Mennonite Board of
Congregational Ministries as Minister of Leadership. Dale
is a member of the Martinsburg congregation in
Allegheny Conference. His wife, Doris, is a psychothera-
pist. They are parents of three adult children.

Anne Stuckey's commitment to and passion for pastoral
ministry has placed her squarely in the Ministerial
Services Office of the Mennonite Board of Congregational
Ministries. In this capacity Anne serves as Minister of
Congregational Leadership, a position she shares with
Dale W. Stoltzfus. Stuckey keeps her feet rooted in the
local congregation, as preaching minister at Salem
Mennonite Church at Waldron, Mich. Two children,
Matthew, 18, and Leah, 16, keep her honest. Her husband
Terry is an Emergency Room Physician Assistant.

Everett J. Thomas has served as president of the
Mennonite Board of Congregational Ministries in Elkhart,
IN, since 1989. MBCM has been an advocate for the
Congregational Discipling Vision since adopting it as a
formal vision for congregational life in the Mennonite
Church in the early 1990s. Everett is a member of the
Walnut Hill Mennonite Church in Goshen, Ind, where he
presently serves as an elder. After a fire destroyed the
church building in 1989, Thomas led the rebuilding
process which sparked his interest in church architecture.
Since that time, Everett and other MBCM staff have led
workshops and seminars on the relationship of

Anabaptist theology and church architecture.

Through his MBCM duties Everett also helped initiate The Giving Project: Growing Faithful Stewards, a five-year stewardship education initiative sponsored by agencies of the Mennonite Church and the General Conference Mennonite Church.